*Ranger Up Presents*

# Mixed Martial Arts IQ:
# The Ultimate Test of True Fandom
# (Volume II)

Zac Robinson

IQ Series books are the trademark of Black Mesa Publishing, LLC.

Cataloging-in-Publication Data is available from the Library of Congress.

ISBN: 9780982675908
First edition, first printing.

Cover designed by and courtesy of Ranger Up.

Black Mesa Publishing, LLC
Florida
David Horne and Marc CB Maxwell
Black.Mesa.Publishing@gmail.com

www.blackmesabooks.com

*For Jace and Xin Ai*

# Contents

# Foreword

It was a hot, miserable Georgia day in 1999 and I was going through the combatives portion of Ranger School at The Home of the Infantry (and armpit of the south), Fort Benning. We were doing throws and I was paired up with the skinniest wannabe Ranger in history when the Instructors suddenly ordered us to throw each other ten times. I gently lifted this kid in the air and placed him as lightly as I could onto the sawdust that was our "mat." Unfortunately, my lack of raw unadulterated testosterone-fueled desire to smash this kid into the ground quickly drew the ire of the only Marine Corps Instructor in the fight pit. "You too scared to throw him, Ranger? Do it again!" Of course, I heeded the Gunnery Sergeant's instructions and gave the next throw a little more "oomph." He was not impressed. "Again!" he shouted. I added a smidge more power, but was still unwilling to chance hurting this kid by hitting him with a full-out makikomi throw. It was at this point that the Gunnery Sergeant, after challenging my sexual orientation in the most creative and impressive ways possible, dropped this fateful line: "Well, okay Ranger! If you're too scared to throw your buddy, then how about you throw me!"

All eyes were now on us.

What this man did not know is that I was, at one point in my life, a high-level Judoka and a pretty decent wrestler. I'm not Karo Parisyan or Josh Koscheck, but if need be I can throw the hell out of someone. I grabbed him like a rag doll and threw him with perfect Uchi Mata while simultaneously leaping in the air so that every ounce of my 194 pounds crashed onto his solar plexus when we both landed on the unforgiving ground. I stood up. He tried to get up but lack of oxygen kept him down.

The moral of the story is that if you only sort of understand something, you can end up looking like a real jackass.

Fast forward to the present day. You're at a bar with ten of your buddies and some new guy you've never met watching the latest UFC. It's Randy Couture versus Chuck Liddell Part Seven and you're all making random drunken bets about who is going to win, when new guy drops, "It's all gonna come down to who has the better jiu jitsu. I hear Couture trained with Royce Gracie, so I think he'll definitely win." Your urge to beat that guy about the head, neck, and shoulders subsides, mostly due to the fact that you just threw up in your mouth from second-hand embarrassment. You vow then and there that you will never be that guy, and rejoice in the fact that you're not some MMA newb.

But how far from him are you, really?

That's what Zac Robinson wants to help you find out. Robinson, the author of *Mixed Martial Arts IQ: The Ultimate Test of True Fandom* and the co-author of *Mixed Martial Arts: An Interactive Guide to the World of Sports,* decided to follow up his two previous fan-favorites with an even more challenging test of your MMA knowledge with *Ranger Up Presents: Mixed Martial Arts IQ (Volume II).* The book is set up in five chapters, with each chapter representing five MMA Fights. You'll be asked a series of ten questions for each fight. Every correct answer gets you one step closer to a first round knockout victory. Every wrong answer ... well, you might find yourself in the Octagon wearing one boxing glove wondering what the hell you just got yourself into.

Robinson spent 14,598 hours researching the most mundane facts about KOs, TKOs, omoplatas, gogoplatas, Fu Manchuplatas, Spandex, missing teeth, fungal infections, and all the unsavory tidbits of MMA life to bring you this book. He asked these hard questions to garner the knowledge that no one else had the guts (and, in a lot of cases, desire) to learn so that you will be equipped to dazzle your friends, avoid personal embarrassment in public MMA party settings, and smite those who would challenge your MMA mastery. No matter what, whether you're a newb or an expert, there is something to learn in this book, and you'll have a hell of a lot of fun doing it.

— *Nick Palmisciano, President, Ranger Up*

# Acknowledgements

More than any project I've ever been involved with, this book showcases the patriotism and respect inherent in the Mixed Martial Arts community for the Armed Forces.

When MMA writer Zac Robinson, who for the past decade has served overseas as a DOD civilian side-by-side with our men and women in uniform, approached us with the idea of raising money for military charities with his third book, we were thrilled to be a part of the effort. Moreover, we were touched that he would donate the time and significant effort it takes to write a book to benefit our troops. Given everything that he had put into this project, we knew we had to provide our best effort. Immediately, we reached out to our great friend, brother in arms, and networking juggernaut Lex McMahon for some help gathering up some great MMA stars to be part of the book. Lex, the son of the late television star and Marine Corps Colonel Ed McMahon, is a Marine. And if you've ever met a Marine before, you realize that once a Marine has a mission, there is no way to stop him while he is still breathing ... and even then it's questionable. Between Ranger Up fighters, our friends in the MMA community, and Lex's inexplicable ability to get every man, woman, and child in the known universe involved, we believe we have put together an incredible array of fighters for this book.

Every one of these fighters volunteered to be part of this book without compensation in order to raise money for the troops and awareness for two great organizations – Soldiers' Angels and Hire Heroes. I don't think you could have found this many top athletes willing to do so in any other sport and it is a credit to each one of these fine gentlemen and the sport of MMA as a whole that they chose to be involved.

For our part, we're thrilled to have played a small role in designing and marketing this work, and we hope we are able to make a difference in the lives of those who served.

Finally, and again, a special thanks to the author, Zac Robinson – his desire to share the fruits of his labor with the military community speaks volumes to his character.

— *Nick Palmisciano, President, Ranger Up*

I'd like to add to Nick's acknowledgements. Lex McMahon has been absolutely instrumental in the process of putting this book together and as Nick mentioned, all the fighters were so willing to jump on board and help out in whatever way they could (you can see a list of those involved in the references). Nick certainly shouldn't short himself or Ranger Up either. When I came to him with the idea of a partnership he recognized the potential and has been great to work with throughout.

This project would not have been possible without Black Mesa's willingness to give up a large chunk of its profits to charity (we're not talking 10% here, closer to 50%). I don't know if any other publisher would do what they have done, especially with the current state of the publishing industry.

Martin McNeil is a great guy who also happens to be one of, if not the, most talented MMA photographers in the business. Remember the bloody Joe Stevenson photo? That was Martin and it is the shot he became known for, but he has taken one great shot after another. I'm not sure how he does it but he captures the emotion of the moment in stunning fashion and you'll find yourself thinking about many of his photos long after you've taken your eyes off of them.

You can find Martin online:
http://flavors.me/martinmcneilphoto

He no doubt has made this book much better than it would've been.

Finally, thanks to all the men and women who serve and their families, and not just in the U.S. Military, but those around the world who have taken the oath to protect our way of life. I hope you enjoy the book.

— *Zac Robinson*

# About Ranger Up

Founded in 2006, Ranger Up is owned and operated by a patriotic group of Army Rangers, Special Forces, and Infantrymen who have stood in combat zones around the world and looked our nation's enemies in the eyes. Their apparel designs are based entirely on the warrior ethos, often depicted through significant military figures throughout history.

The company is committed to giving back to its brothers and sisters in arms in the Armed Forces, Police, Fire, and first responders. They believe wholeheartedly that MMA saves lives on the battlefield and on the streets. In the past year alone they've visited Iraq and multiple bases throughout the U.S. while founding and executing the Train the Troops MMA program, and presented at the Pentagon regarding the benefits of MMA in an effort to increase the survivability of our troops. They also regularly visit Walter Reed and other military hospitals with their sponsored fighters to raise morale among our nation's wounded.

In addition to supporting MMA on the battlefield, Ranger Up supports MMA in the cage by sponsoring top-level veteran fighters like Tim Kennedy, Jorge Rivera, Brian Stann, Kris McCray, and Tim Credeur, while supporting dozens of up-and-coming military veterans and non-military patriots in smaller shows around the U.S.

Ranger Up isn't simply an apparel company, but an extension of the warrior ethos and lifestyle. To give more of our nation's warriors a voice so they can tell the (often humorous) stories of those who serve, they founded the Rhino Den (www.rhinoden.com), now one of the largest patriotic content sites in existence. Supporting military authors is the next natural step, and they are honored to be a part of this book.

# Introduction

This has to be one of the most unique books ever to find its way into print. It is the result of a partnership between Ranger Up and Black Mesa Publishing to put together a great product for MMA fans and to raise awareness and help two worthy organizations, Soldiers' Angels and Hire Heroes USA, through donating a significant portion of the proceeds.

Soldiers' Angels is a non-profit organization that provides aid to U.S. service members and their families. It was started by Patti Patton-Bader, the mom of two soldiers, in 2003 and has done a tremendous amount of good since. Soldiers' Angels volunteers have written letters and sent care packages to deployed service members, provided voice controlled/adaptive laptops to nearly 3,000 wounded service members, and provided Level III Kevlar armored blankets to give personnel extra protection while in their vehicles. And this is just the tip of the iceberg. You can join and learn more about Soldiers' Angels online.

Hire Heroes USA came about in June of 2007 and MMA star Brian Stann is the Executive Director. It is a non-profit organization that's focus is to help veterans get jobs. It operates at no cost to veterans or hiring companies and its service is desperately needed. As of late 2009, the veteran unemployment rate was about 3 percentage points higher than the national average. As Stann says, "You can't train honor, courage, and commitment." You can learn more about Hire Heroes USA and how to be a part of it online as well.

The final reason we call this book so unique is because it is full of Mixed Martial Arts history and trivia, and it is one big challenge to MMA fans worldwide. Each set of ten questions represent a fight and depending on how well you do in answering the questions determines your fate. You might win big with a KO or sub, or lose in brutal fashion by knees in the clinch. By the end of the book you'll have a 25-fight record and will know exactly where you stand, a can, a contender, or maybe even the greatest of all-time ... Good luck!

Ranger Up's Tribute to the Fearless
Leader Genghis Khan

# Ranger Up Presents
## Mixed Martial Arts IQ

---

## Round One

Everyone has to start somewhere. These first five fights represent the start of your career. Train hard and fight well or you'll have to go back to serving burgers at McDonalds.

# BUILDING AN EMPIRE

ONE MAN TOOK FRAGMENTED PARTS and put them together to create a whole that in turn built an Empire. He was born Temujin, meaning "ironworker" and it was fitting. He had to have an iron will and had to see a vision that nobody else could in order to forge his near indestructible force.

He united his nomadic people as he defeated one tribe after another and then brought them into his. Loyalty and merit, not family ties, gave his soldiers power. He promised and delivered future riches from war victories and with each victory he became stronger.

Once the tribes were united, Temujin became known as Genghis Khan and he unleashed hell on his enemies. He did so by gathering intelligence and then adapting his plan of attack. Often he outsmarted his enemies and then ruthlessly destroyed them.

Thanks to Genghis Khan, in less than a hundred years the Mongols conquered much of Asia and Eastern Europe.

Now some 800 years later we can see that Mixed Martial Artists must have many of the same characteristics as Genghis Khan. The modern day sport fighter has to have vision and an iron will. He has to trust his team and he has to gain knowledge before he can expect to bring his vision to fruition, and even then victory is never a guarantee, his empire may never be built.

Then there's us fans. Are we like the great and ruthless Genghis Khan? Not really, but we do love gathering intelligence. We do love knowing more about the sport than our counterparts. And this is why you are holding Ranger Up's MMA IQ. It is a path toward that fighting spirit, a vessel that will either help you build your empire one answer at a time or vanquish you and leave those dear to you bathed in tears...

## FIGHT NUMBER 1

## AT THE JACKSON COUNTY AUTO SHOW
## (CARS AND KO'S)

QUESTION 1: The Ultimate Fighting Championship was dreamed up by Art Davie, Rorion Gracie and Bob Meyrowitz. It pitted men from various martial arts backgrounds competing in a single elimination tournament. The first was on November 12, 1993 in this city.
   a)   Detroit, Michigan
   b)   Los Angeles, California
   c)   Denver, Colorado
   d)   Tulsa, Oklahoma

QUESTION 2: Remembering the city might be pretty easy, but in which arena was the event held? It was torn down in 1999.
   a)   Cobo Arena
   b)   McNichols Arena
   c)   The Pepsi Center
   d)   The Staples Center

QUESTION 3: We all know that Royce Gracie stormed through the first UFC tournament by beating the one-gloved Art Jimmerson, Ken Shamrock, and then Gerard Gordeau and in the process he introduced the world to Gracie Jiu Jitsu. How much money did he earn for winning the tournament?
   a)   $5,000
   b)   $25,000
   c)   $50,000
   d)   $100,000

QUESTION 4: This UFC fighter got off to a 2-1 start with the promotion and was awarded the Silver Star for his actions as the 2nd Mobile Assault Platoon Leader of Weapons Company in Karabilah, Iraq in 2005. He is also the Executive Director of Hire Heroes USA (www.hireheroesusa.org).
   a)   Tim Kennedy
   b)   Brian Stann
   c)   Brandon Vera
   d)   Damien Stelly

**QUESTION 5:** Through 50 fights Gilbert Yvel had an impressive 36-13-1 record, but three of those losses were due to disqualification. Back in 1998 Yvel was DQ'd for biting, in 2001 he was DQ'd for gouging Don Frye's eyes, and in 2004 he was DQ'd against Atte Backman for this reason.
 a) he KO'd the referee
 b) he both bit and gouged Backman
 c) he punched Backman in the testicles six times
 d) he tried to choke Backman with the bottom rope

**QUESTION 6:** At UFC Fight Night 19, Brian Stann, Nate Quarry, Carlos Condit, Gray Maynard, and Nate Diaz were all victorious. Someone that didn't see these wins, at least not in person, was UFC commentator Joe Rogan. He was out so this man stepped in to take his place.
 a) Frank Mir
 b) Kenny Florian
 c) Miguel Torres
 d) Stephan Bonnar

**QUESTION 7:** Former wrestlers and current UFC stars Gray Maynard and Rashad Evans were roommates when on the road during college. They kept the scale in their room for the guys to check their weights and Gray tells a hilarious story.

Courtesy of Gray Maynard.

"Around 3 or 4am someone came in our room and crawled into my bed. I thought it was a teammate that had to cut a lot of weight and was tired, so I turned over to kick him out and it was a guy I'd never seen before that smelled like alcohol. I jumped up and woke up Rashad, we both were yelling at the guy to get up. He woke up to a big black man (Rashad) and me (at the time I had my front teeth knocked out). He looked at us like we were in his room! The guy was naked and tried to put MY clothes on. We were throwing towels and slapping his hands off my clothes. Finally we got a knock on the door and it was his wife or girlfriend. She opened the door and didn't say a word, just looked completely shocked and pulled him out of our room. After it was all done we laughed pretty hard." This happened at Illinois, but Gray and Rashad wrestled at this university.

    a)   Ohio State
    b)   Michigan
    c)   Michigan State
    d)   Northwestern

**QUESTION 8:** This Strikeforce middleweight champ relinquished the belt because he took time away from the cage in 2009 to focus on his acting career. He did return in December and dominated for most of the fight before suffering a shocking KO for his first career loss.

    a)   Jake Shields
    b)   Robbie Lawler
    c)   Cung Le
    d)   Frank Shamrock

**QUESTION 9:** One of the most heinous fouls in UFC history came at UFC 43 when Wes Sims (who was a contestant on *The Ultimate Fighter* Season 10) stomped on the head of this fighter. The two fought again and Sims was on the losing end of a KO.

    a)   Frank Mir
    b)   Kimo Leopoldo
    c)   Mike Kyle
    d)   Tim Sylvia

**QUESTION 10:** What did Quinton "Rampage" Jackson say when he was asked where he saw himself in two years?

    a)   "I see myself in a Japanese penthouse with many Japanese women."

    b)   "Well, right now I'm 23. So in two years I see myself 25."

    c)   "With the belt around my waist and wads of cash in my pocket."

    d)   "I don't know where I'll be in two days. How can you ask me about two years?"

## ANSWER KEY FOR YOUR MMA DEBUT
## (CARS AND KO'S)

| QUESTION 1: | C | | QUESTION 6: | B |
|---|---|---|---|---|
| QUESTION 2: | B | | QUESTION 7: | C |
| QUESTION 3: | C | | QUESTION 8: | C |
| QUESTION 4: | B | | QUESTION 9: | A |
| QUESTION 5: | A | | QUESTION 10: | B |

## FIGHT RESULTS

| 10 for 10 | = Flying knee KO victory in 9 seconds |
|---|---|
| 9 for 10 | = Guillotine choke victory in 22 seconds |
| 8 for 10 | = Unanimous decision victory |
| 7 for 10 | = Split decision victory |
| 6 for 10 | = Split decision loss |
| 5 for 10 | = Unanimous decision loss |
| 4 or fewer | = KO'd by ground and pound |

## FIGHT RECORD

| Wins: | ____ | | Losses: | ____ |
|---|---|---|---|---|
| KO's: | ____ | | KO's: | ____ |
| Subs: | ____ | | Subs: | ____ |
| Decisions: | ____ | | Decisions: | ____ |

# FIGHT NUMBER 2

## AT THE SOUTHSIDE HOOTERS
## (WINGS, WHOOPINGS, AND WOMEN)

QUESTION 11: While recovering from a broken jaw suffered in a June 2004 fight with Chris Leben, this fighter happened to be at a Vancouver, Washington restaurant when an armed gunman tried to hold up the place. He quickly disarmed the gunman and knocked him out.
   a) Matt Lindland
   b) Matt Hume
   c) Ryan Schultz
   d) Benji Radach

QUESTION 12: Yushin Okami and Anderson Silva fought at Rumble on the Rock 8 in Hawaii on January 20, 2006. Okami got the win due to this reason.
   a) DQ due to an illegal upkick
   b) submission due to flying scissor heel hook
   c) an unintentional eye poke that forced the bout's stoppage
   d) a horrible decision by the judges

QUESTION 13: After UFC 84 Tito Ortiz left the UFC and it looked as if he might fight for Strikeforce or Affliction. In the end he didn't fight for either, so through 23 fights and a 15-7-1 record how many times did Ortiz fight outside of the UFC?
   a) never
   b) once
   c) twice
   d) three times

QUESTION 14: Sticking with Tito Ortiz, his fight at UFC 84 came against this man and Ortiz suffered a tough loss despite almost pulling out a miraculous submission in the final moments.
   a) Ken Shamrock
   b) Lyoto Machida
   c) Chuck Liddell
   d) Forrest Griffin

**QUESTION 15:** New Japan Pro Wrestler Yuji Nagata suffered through two TKO's during his short-lived MMA career (it lasted a total of 1:23) but it is hard to blame him considering his two opponents were ... which pair?

    a)   Don Frye and Alistair Overeem
    b)   Wanderlei Silva and Quinton Jackson
    c)   Antonio Rodrigo Nogueira and Mauricio Rua
    d)   Fedor Emelianenko and Mirko "Cro Cop" Filipovic

**QUESTION 16:** Chael Sonnen is a unique fighter with a unique name. His mom, Claudia, liked the name Michael but was afraid people would call him Mike (not that there's anything wrong with that) so she decided to drop the "Mi" and came up with Chael. It worked well for the UFC star who was also a two-time National Champion for this University.

    a)   Washington
    b)   Boise State
    c)   Oregon
    d)   Oregon State

Chael Sonnen – courtesy of Martin McNeil.

**QUESTION 17:** Staying with Chael Sonnen, while he was winning National Championships he also earned a degree in this field of study.
   a)   Sociology
   b)   Physical Education
   c)   Communication
   d)   Art History

**QUESTION 18:** This former PRIDE fighter made his UFC debut at 76 against Lyoto Machida and carried an umbrella to the Octagon, lost a decision, and then tested positive for marijuana. He fought one more time for the promotion, at UFC 84, before heading back to Japan as a mainstay for Sengoku.
   a)   Yuki Kondo
   b)   Ryo Chonan
   c)   Kazuhiro Nakamura
   d)   Akihiro Gono

**QUESTION 19:** In 2007 this man shocked everyone by KO'ing Antonio Rogerio Nogueira and Ricardo Arona in brutal fashion at PRIDE 33 and PRIDE 34. With a ton of hype he entered the UFC where he went 1-2 before being released.
   a)   Wanderlei Silva
   b)   Mauricio Rua
   c)   Rameau Thierry Sokoudjou
   d)   Quinton Jackson

**QUESTION 20:** This man appeared on *The Ultimate Fighter* Season four and beat Jorge Rivera and Edwin DeWees. When asked about being on the show and fighting without a crowd he said, "It was strange, like fighting in your backyard. But if asked again I'd do it tomorrow. It was great ... training twice a day with some of the best in the world, living in a five million dollar mansion, eating a thirty-buck steak everyday and I got paid to do it, wow!"
   a)   Shonie Carter
   b)   Rich Clementi
   c)   Patrick Cote
   d)   Gideon Ray

## Answer Key for Fight Number 2
## (Wings, Whoopings, and Women)

| | | | | |
|---|---|---|---|---|
| **Question 11:** | D | | **Question 16:** | C |
| **Question 12:** | A | | **Question 17:** | A |
| **Question 13:** | B | | **Question 18:** | C |
| **Question 14:** | B | | **Question 19:** | C |
| **Question 15:** | D | | **Question 20:** | C |

## Fight Results

| | |
|---|---|
| 10 for 10 | = Win by Arm Triangle sub in 42 seconds |
| 9 for 10 | = KO win due to slam at 1:03 of round one |
| 8 for 10 | = Unanimous decision victory |
| 7 for 10 | = Split decision victory |
| 6 for 10 | = Split decision loss |
| 5 for 10 | = Unanimous decision loss |
| 4 or fewer | = You got head kick KO'd |

## Fight Record

| Wins: | _____ | Losses: | _____ |
|---|---|---|---|
| KO's: | _____ | KO's: | _____ |
| Subs: | _____ | Subs: | _____ |
| Decisions: | _____ | Decisions: | _____ |

## FIGHT NUMBER 3

## AT THE AREA 51 FESTIVAL
## (ALIENS AND ARMBARS)

QUESTION 21: Through 49 fights and a 27-17-5 record, Chris "Lights Out" Lytle had never had his lights put out. He had lost twice due to being cut. The first was at UFC 55 when he was cut by Joe Riggs and the second came against this tough welterweight at UFC 78.
  a) Josh Koscheck
  b) Thiago Alves
  c) Matt Hughes
  d) Robbie Lawler

QUESTION 22: This fighter was on *The Ultimate Fighter* Season 2 where he fought and lost to Melvin Guillard on the Finale in Las Vegas. He then fought three more times in the United States and seven times overseas, before returning to Las Vegas at UFC 106 where he lost once again.
  a) Marcus Davis
  b) Michael Bisping
  c) Jorge Gurgel
  d) Joe Stevenson

QUESTION 23: Former Navy SEAL, pro wrestler, and governor of Minnesota Jesse Ventura defended Mixed Martial Arts quite well on this talk show. He said among other things, "I think its [MMA] very professionally run ... they're honorable, they're respectful..."
  a) Oprah Winfrey
  b) Larry King
  c) Bill O'Reilly
  d) The View

QUESTION 24: Matt Lindland began his collegiate wrestling career at Clackamas Community College in Oregon and claimed the 158 pound NJCAA championship in 1991. He was then recruited by numerous colleges and fell in love with this school during his first visit. He was ready to sign, but head coach Tim Neumann told him

to go ahead and take the rest of his recruiting trips to make sure. Matt did, but came back to this school.
a)   University of Oregon
b)   Oklahoma State University
c)   Iowa State University
d)   University of Nebraska

**QUESTION 25:** Apparently UFC heavyweight Brock Lesnar would rather drink this beer, even though Bud Light is one of the promotion's main sponsors.
a)   Miller Lite
b)   Michelob
c)   Coors Light
d)   Keystone Light

**QUESTION 26:** The first UFC super fight happened at UFC 5 and featured these two men. It was highly anticipated and had a time limit of 30 minutes that was pushed to 31 minutes and finally ended at 36 minutes. The super fight turned out not to be so super, it ended in a draw because there were no judges.
a)   Dan Severn and Oleg Taktarov
b)   Ken Shamrock and Royce Gracie
c)   Royce Gracie and Tank Abbott
d)   Ken Shamrock and Dan Severn

**QUESTION 27:** Staying with the early UFC's and long fights, it was at Ultimate Ultimate 95 when these two men fought for 18 minutes and then the judges rendered the first decision in the history of the UFC.
a)   Tank Abbott and Steve Jennum (Abbott won)
b)   Dan Severn and Tank Abbott (Severn won)
c)   Marco Ruas and Keith Hackney (Ruas won)
d)   Oleg Taktarov and Dave Beneteau (Taktarov won)

**QUESTION 28:** It was at UFC 74 when Renato Sobral held an Anaconda choke on this opponent after he tapped and after referee Steve Mazzagatti told him to release it and then attempted to break the hold. Sobral was defiant afterward because after the weigh in his opponent said, "You're going down mother-********." Sobral told Joe Rogan, "He has to learn respect. He deserved that. He called me

mother-******."
   a) David Heath
   b) Jason Lambert
   c) Chael Sonnen
   d) Travis Wiuff

**QUESTION 29:** In what way was Sobral punished for holding the choke after his opponent tapped?
   a) he wasn't punished and is still fighting in the UFC
   b) he was fined $2,500 and suspended for three months
   c) half of his purse or $25,000 was withheld and he was released from the UFC
   d) he had to spend five straight days in a room with a video loop of the crowd reactions at an Oprah Winfrey show when she gives them a big prize while at the same time repeatedly listening to Whitney Houston's version of *I Will Always Love You*

**QUESTION 30:** Patrick "The Predator" Cote earned his nickname because of his willingness to learn.

Patrick Cote – courtesy of Martin McNeil.

As he said, "I always wanted more and more and more." He got a lot in what was no doubt one of the best fights in the history of MMA in Canada when he beat this man by rear naked choke in the fifth round of MFC 9 for the middleweight title. Cote said of his opponent and the fight, "He is no joke! It was the kind of fight where afterward you get better and better because it was such a war."

  a)  Bill Mahood
  b)  Jason Day
  c)  Carlos Newton
  d)  Jason MacDonald

## ANSWER KEY FOR FIGHT NUMBER 3
## (ALIENS AND ARMBARS)

| QUESTION 21: | B | QUESTION 26: | B |
| QUESTION 22: | A | QUESTION 27: | B |
| QUESTION 23: | B | QUESTION 28: | A |
| QUESTION 24: | D | QUESTION 29: | C |
| QUESTION 25: | C | QUESTION 30: | D |

## FIGHT RESULTS

| 10 for 10 | = KO win by brutal overhand right |
| 9 for 10 | = Kneebar in round two for the win |
| 8 for 10 | = Unanimous decision victory |
| 7 for 10 | = Split decision victory |
| 6 for 10 | = Split decision loss |
| 5 for 10 | = Unanimous decision loss |
| 4 or fewer | = You got cut bad and RNC'd to sleep |

## FIGHT RECORD

| Wins: | _____ | Losses: | _____ |
| KO's: | _____ | KO's: | _____ |
| Subs: | _____ | Subs: | _____ |
| Decisions: | _____ | Decisions: | _____ |

## FIGHT NUMBER 4

## AT THE SAN DIMAS COMMUNITY COLLEGE CATHOLIC GIRLS SCHOOL
## (FISTS AND FLIRTS)

QUESTION 31: At PRIDE 33 Nick Diaz won in shocking fashion by submitting this fighter with a Gogoplata. The fight was one of the greatest ever, but afterward Diaz's win was changed to a no contest by the Nevada State Athletic Commission because he tested positive for marijuana.
- a) Koji Oishi
- b) Mike Aina
- c) Eddie Bravo
- d) Takanori Gomi

QUESTION 32: Nick Diaz's Gogoplata submission was only the second in PRIDE's near ten year history. The first came just months earlier when this fighter subbed Joachim Hansen at PRIDE Shockwave in Japan.
- a) Tatsuya Kawajiri
- b) Hayato Sakurai
- c) Eddie Alvarez
- d) Shinya Aoki

QUESTION 33: During an interview with Raw Vegas, this fighter kicked VP Eric Newby in the leg. Newby limped and the fighter said, "It's not that bad." Reportedly Newby was later treated for a hair-line fracture of the femur. Denise Pernula who was conducting the interview said, "He deserved it," toward the end of the clip. In another interview, this one with UFC Junkie (now MMA Junkie), this fighter was asked if he broke Newby's leg and he said with a laugh, "Our lawyer told me not to answer any questions regarding that. No, no, I didn't, and he's a big ham. But I mean if he comes back I'll be happy to try again."
- a) Quinton Jackson
- b) Junie Browning
- c) Forrest Griffin
- d) Pat Barry

**QUESTION 34:** In April of 2009 Kyle Maynard lost an amateur fight to Brian Fry at Auburn Fight Night. Even with the loss it was pretty amazing because Kyle ...
  a)  is legally blind
  b)  was in a horrific car wreck and not expected to wake from a coma just one year to the day of the fight
  c)  does not have arms past his elbows or legs
  d)  had kicked a long time heroin addiction that left him with a constant twitch in his right shoulder

**QUESTION 35:** This UFC star talked of his propensity for drinking his urine every morning as a therapy. When asked what it tasted like he said it was sour if he eats a lot of protein the day before and sweet if he eats a lot of carbohydrates. Forrest Griffin, when asked about it, said, "I haven't been able to secure any of [this fighter's] pee. I think I'd really drink it though, I think I would. I would do anything for this sport but quit coffee."
  a)  Anderson Silva
  b)  Lyoto Machida
  c)  Brock Lesnar
  d)  B.J. Penn

**QUESTION 36:** When asked if he thought he looked like Jim Carrey and if he was a fan, UFC star Rich Franklin said, "Maybe a little, but some people seem to think we look like twins. I have been hearing it since he was on *In Living Color*. I would say I am a fan, I thought his last movie, *Yes Man*, didn't get the credit it deserved."

Rich Franklin – courtesy of Martin McNeil.

Rich deserves credit for his role in this charity that raises money for groups that fight against violence. "We have 'American Fighter' parties at several UFC fights to help raise money," Rich said. "We've helped domestic violence groups as well as bullying programs." And the name of the charity is ...
 a) Keep it in the Ring
 b) The Ace Foundation
 c) Fighters KO'ing Violence
 d) Only in the Octagon

**QUESTION 37:** These brothers were just a year away from finishing law school, but they decided to quit and pursue their MMA careers. Most would say it worked out okay.
 a) The Emelianenko's
 b) The Overeem's
 c) The Lauzon's
 d) The Nogueira's

**QUESTION 38:** It is believed that this man is the first to actually thank his hairdresser after a victory. At UFC 99, while talking to Joe Rogan he threw into his thank you, "and um, Ben, my hairdresser," then pointed to his head.
 a) Clay Guida
 b) Dan Hardy
 c) Amir Sadollah
 d) Keith Jardine

**QUESTION 39:** Russian Viacheslav Datsik was pretty much a complete mad man at each of his fights. His last bout came in 2003 and according to Sherdog he finished at 4-9 with six straight losses. He got a KO in his debut though against this future UFC heavyweight champ who was also making his debut at M-1 MFC World Championship 1999.
 a) Andrei Arlovski
 b) Kevin Randleman
 c) Ricco Rodriguez
 d) Frank Mir

**QUESTION 40:** Nate Quarry did not really begin training until he was 24 years old, a very late start for a fighter but he's managed just fine. Why did he get such a late start to his MMA career?

a) He had aspirations of competing in the Winter Olympics as a speed skater
b) He lived in a tree house community named Finca Bella Vista in a Costa Rican rain forest until he was 20
c) He spent 21 months in prison for skimming money from the Jiffy Lube (his employer while completing college)
d) He grew up as a Jehovah Witness

## ANSWER KEY FOR FIGHT NUMBER 4
## (FISTS AND FLIRTS)

| | | | |
|---|---|---|---|
| QUESTION 31: | D | QUESTION 36: | A |
| QUESTION 32: | D | QUESTION 37: | D |
| QUESTION 33: | C | QUESTION 38: | B |
| QUESTION 34: | C | QUESTION 39: | A |
| QUESTION 35: | B | QUESTION 40: | D |

## FIGHT RESULTS

| | |
|---|---|
| 10 for 10 | = Guillotine choke sub in 13 seconds |
| 9 for 10 | = Liver kick KO |
| 8 for 10 | = Unanimous decision victory |
| 7 for 10 | = Split decision victory |
| 6 for 10 | = Split decision loss |
| 5 for 10 | = Unanimous decision loss |
| 4 or fewer | = You were subbed via Kimura |

## FIGHT RECORD

Wins:          _____              Losses:          _____

KO's:          _____              KO's:            _____

Subs:          _____              Subs:            _____

Decisions:     _____              Decisions:       _____

## FIGHT NUMBER 5

## AT THE LUCKY STAR CASINO
## (GAMBLE WITH YOUR FISTS)

QUESTION 41: At UFC Ultimate Fight Night 17 this fighter was underneath Mac Danzig when he tried to punch the side of Danzig's head and instead punched himself ... *twice*. Despite the self-inflicted ground and pound he went on to win the exciting fight by triangle choke in round two. Unfortunately for him he dropped his next two fights and was released from the UFC.
a)  Josh Neer
b)  Clay Guida
c)  Jim Miller
d)  Nate Diaz

QUESTION 42: In August of 2009 Amanda Haney and Brenda Robinson fought at the Bay City Hooters. The fight was odd for this reason.
a)  they are mother and daughter
b)  they were fighting over a man who also happened to be the referee and had also just won a wing-eating contest where he downed 89 three mile island wings
c)  the winner (Haney) was actually hired to work at the Bay City Hooters as reward for the victory
d)  it was the fifth time they fought each other and both of them had eight fights overall heading into the bout

QUESTION 43: After his brutal KO of Akihiro Gono at Sengoku Ninth Battle, this fighter said, "Yeah, as soon as that kick landed, his body went stiff, stumbled two steps and fell into the ropes. I knew as soon as it landed, it was over. That's why I didn't continue the attack."
a)  Kazuo Misaki
b)  Dan Hornbuckle
c)  Dan Henderson
d)  Denis Kang

QUESTION 44: July 20, 2009 was a pretty good night for this man. First he caught Hayato Sakurai with a head kick and finished him with punches, and then he KO'd Jason High with a head kick to win Dream's 2009 Welterweight Grand Prix Championship and become the promotion's first welterweight champ.

    a)   Andre Galvao
    b)   Che Mills
    c)   Shinya Aoki
    d)   Marius Zaromskis

**QUESTION 45:** "I was always gonna fight regardless the outcome of the Olympic Trials," King Mo Lawal said. "My dream was to be a MMA champion! The transition was pretty easy because this was something I always wanted to do and I was a student of the MMA game." King Mo was a late replacement at this event and fought what many thought would be a stiff test in Travis Wiuff for his MMA debut. Mo TKO'd him in just over two minutes though. "I'd been training for about a month," King Mo said. "The feeling of stepping into the ring was the best feeling I've ever experienced. It felt like I knocked someone out before I fought!" At what event did this take place?

    a)   YAMMA Pit Fighting
    b)   Sengoku 3
    c)   DREAM 6 MWGP
    d)   Sengoku 5

Courtesy of King Mo Lawal.

**QUESTION 46:** This UFC middleweight said of his jump into MMA, "When I showed up for practice one day everybody was wearing MMA gloves instead of wrestling shoes. They had a pair for me, so I joined in. We were in the back of a car lot at the time. It wasn't a team or even a gym. It was just a space with a mat." It turned out to be a good decision as after his dominating victory at UFC 104 he was ranked in 7th place in the Middleweight division by the Independent World MMA Rankings and he climbed the ladder from there.
   a)  Dan Henderson
   b)  Jorge Rivera
   c)  Chael Sonnen
   d)  Vitor Belfort

**QUESTION 47:** Steve Ramirez had demonstrated a propensity for fast fights. Through 12 he only had one make it into the second round and four didn't even pass the two minute mark. Then there's his fight with Darvin Wattree on July 25, 2009 at Pure Combat 9. It was ridiculous because ...
   a)  Wattree subbed Ramirez with a Guillotine in seven seconds
   b)  Wattree and Ramirez KO'd each other with overhand rights ten seconds into the fight
   c)  Ramirez KO'd Wattree in only 3 seconds
   d)  Ramirez "KO'd" Wattree in 5 seconds but then it was decided that it was stopped early so Ramirez KO'd Wattree a second time only 24 seconds into the fight

**QUESTION 48:** Not long after graduating from this university with a degree in economics, Dan Cramer was on *The Ultimate Fighter* Season 7 where he fought his way onto the show and then beat Luke Zachrich before being heel hooked by Tim Credeur. He attended the ...
   a)  University of Tennessee
   b)  University of Arizona
   c)  University of Connecticut
   d)  Phoenix University

**QUESTION 49:** Reportedly Kurt Pellegrino wore this type of shirt to a wrestling tournament, won, and then wore it to all his

tournaments as a lucky shirt ... which earned him this nickname.
a)  Batman
b)  Pedro (It was a "Vote for Pedro" shirt)
c)  Bash Brother  (It was an old Jose Canseco/Mark McGwire Bash Brothers shirt where they are sleeveless with baseball bats over their shoulders)
d)  Cartman

**QUESTION 50:** Who was the referee when Kevin "Kimbo Slice" Ferguson popped James Thompson's ear at Elite XC *Primetime* in front of over 5 million viewers.
a)  John McCarthy
b)  Yves Lavigne
c)  Dan Miragliotta
d)  Herb Dean

## ANSWER KEY FOR FIGHT NUMBER 5
## (GAMBLE WITH YOUR FISTS)

| QUESTION 41: | A | | QUESTION 46: | C |
|---|---|---|---|---|
| QUESTION 42: | A | | QUESTION 47: | C |
| QUESTION 43: | B | | QUESTION 48: | C |
| QUESTION 44: | D | | QUESTION 49: | A |
| QUESTION 45: | D | | QUESTION 50: | C |

## FIGHT RESULTS

| 10 for 10 | = KO win with a Hendo Overhand right |
|---|---|
| 9 for 10 | = Standing RNC finish for the win |
| 8 for 10 | = Unanimous decision victory |
| 7 for 10 | = Split decision victory |
| 6 for 10 | = Split decision loss |
| 5 for 10 | = Unanimous decision loss |
| 4 or fewer | = You were KO'd by a spinning back kick |

## FIGHT RECORD

| Wins: | _____ | Losses: | _____ |
|---|---|---|---|
| KO's: | _____ | KO's: | _____ |
| Subs: | _____ | Subs: | _____ |
| Decisions: | _____ | Decisions: | _____ |

Ranger Up's Homage to the Fiercest of the Viking Warriors

# Round Two

The first leg of your career is over. You're figuring out that you really want to be a fighter. It's time to go all in and get serious about training and fighting.

# BERSERKERS AND VALHALLA

ONLY DEATH IN COMBAT could earn entry into Valhalla "Hall of the Slain" where afterlife would be enjoyed next to the God Odin. This is what the Vikings believed and Odin was the chief God in Norse paganism. He was associated with wisdom, battle, victory, death, and the hunt.

The word Berserker means fighting with a total disregard for one's own well being. It comes from the fiercest of the Vikings, wild warriors so savage they draped their bodies in bear skins. The name berserker likely stems from bjorn "bear" and serkr "shirt."

Upon going berserk, these Vikings were feared by all, friends and enemies, as they would howl like wild animals, bite their shields, and destroy anyone and anything that crossed their path. Their combat training was complete, their savageness was total unreason, their fate was victory followed by exhaustion, or death followed by a trip to Valhalla.

In today's combat, whether in battle or sport, going berserk is not necessarily a good thing. A man has to keep his wits about him even in dire circumstances. The key is to capture some of that berserker mentality or spirit, while remaining intelligent.

Mixed Martial Artists often say things like they are "ready to die in the cage" or that they "are ready to fight to the death." Their words could be better chosen as what they are really saying is that they will enter combat with that Berserker mentality. They will fight without fear of the results.

Those of us who watch these trained men become intelligent Berserkers inside a cage or ring appreciate the total effort. We strive to know all we can about each strike and submission, each victor and defeated, so we can go berserk on our fellow fans with our MMA knowledge and ensure that we will never be pillaged and plundered...

## FIGHT NUMBER 6

## AT THE MINNESOTA STATE FAIR ANNEX NUMBER THREE
## (FISTS-TOGETHER)

**QUESTION 51:** This future star drove almost 12 hours to see UFC 28 and while there he bumped into Pat Miletich. Pat told him he was "a big son of a bitch" and asked him if he did any fighting. He replied that he did a little but had a hard time finding training partners. Pat invited him out to Iowa and he decided to give it a shot.
- a) Tim Sylvia
- b) Ben Rothwell
- c) Drew McFedries
- d) Mike Ciesnolevicz

**QUESTION 52:** In 2005, this former University of Oklahoma wrestler appeared on VH1's reality TV show *Kept*, where he tried to win the affections of Jerry Hall (Mick Jagger's ex) so he could be her "Kept" man. He didn't have such luck and was eliminated in 10th place out of 12 contestants.
- a) Frank Trigg
- b) Jason Miller
- c) Josh Koscheck
- d) Mike Swick

**QUESTION 53:** The clothing company Hoelzer Reich had become a controversial sponsor of numerous MMA fighters for its shirts with depictions of what many believe to be symbols linked to Nazi Germany. This fighter, who was making his official UFC debut, was the last to wear one of the t-shirts to the Octagon as the Zuffa-owned UFC and WEC (and Strikeforce) banned the shirts following *The Ultimate Fighter* Season 10 Finale.
- a) Roy Nelson
- b) Joe Brammer
- c) Matt Mitrione
- d) Justin Wren

**QUESTION 54:** Also on *The Ultimate Fighter* Season 10 Finale, Jon Jones pummeled Matt Hamill with strikes from the mount, but one appeared to be from an illegal "12 to 6" downward elbow. This referee saw that Hamill could not continue and became the first to use instant replay since the Nevada State Athletic Commission began allowing it when he checked to determine if the strike contributed to Hamill's inability to continue. He ruled it did and Jones was disqualified.

a) Steve Mazzagatti
b) John McCarthy
c) Dan Miragliotta
d) Yves Lavigne

**QUESTION 55:** MMA star Brian Stann was born in Japan and grew up in Pennsylvania. He went on to the Naval Academy where he played linebacker and earned a degree in Economics. Back in Pennsylvania he played this position instead of linebacker and set numerous records.

a) Running Back
b) Defensive End
c) Tight End
d) Quarterback

Courtesy of Brian Stann.

**QUESTION 56:** UFC President Dana White once said of this fighter, "For the money he wanted, he's not worth it. He's not a big pay-per-view star, he's not a big attraction, and he's not going to sell out arenas. He wants way too much and he doesn't bring anything to the table."
   a)   Fedor Emelianenko
   b)   Randy Couture
   c)   Dan Henderson
   d)   Matt Lindland

**QUESTION 57:** Tito Ortiz met former porn star Jenna Jameson on My Space and the two began a relationship. Ortiz even cancelled a 2006 appearance as a guest of honor at the United States Marine Corp ball because Jameson was not allowed to attend as his guest. In 2009 Jenna gave birth to twins and they were given the following names.
   a)   Jacob and Jordan
   b)   Jasper and Julissia
   c)   Jesse and Journey
   d)   Joe and Mike

**QUESTION 58:** With his victory at UFC 105, it was set for this man to become the first Brit to fight for a UFC belt.
   a)   Michael Bisping
   b)   Dan Hardy
   c)   Ross Pearson
   d)   Paul Daley

**QUESTION 59:** It was at this event in February of 2006 when Randy Couture first retired from the sport. He opens his book, *Becoming the Natural*, with his feelings going into this fight against Chuck Liddell in a chapter titled *Saying Goodbye*. As we know he returned to fight many more times.
   a)   UFC 49
   b)   UFC 52
   c)   UFC 54
   d)   UFC 57

**QUESTION 60:** Since we mentioned Randy and his brief retirement, it was at this event when he returned as a heavyweight and took on Tim Sylvia. And since we mentioned his book, in it he talks of how

Tim was a little taken aback at Randy's desire to fight him since he'd helped Randy remodel his house a few years before the fight.
   a)  UFC 68
   b)  UFC 70
   c)  UFC 74
   d)  UFC 76

## ANSWER KEY FOR FIGHT NUMBER 6
## (FISTS-TOGETHER)

| | | | | |
|---|---|---|---|---|
| QUESTION 51: | A | | QUESTION 56: | C |
| QUESTION 52: | A | | QUESTION 57: | C |
| QUESTION 53: | B | | QUESTION 58: | B |
| QUESTION 54: | A | | QUESTION 59: | D |
| QUESTION 55: | D | | QUESTION 60: | A |

## FIGHT RESULTS

| | |
|---|---|
| 10 for 10 | = TKO by dominance until stoppage from a nasty cut |
| 9 for 10 | = Win by blood-squirting rear naked choke |
| 8 for 10 | = Unanimous decision victory |
| 7 for 10 | = Split decision victory |
| 6 for 10 | = Split decision loss |
| 5 for 10 | = Unanimous decision loss |
| 4 or fewer | = Subbed by Toe Hold |

## FIGHT RECORD

| | | | |
|---|---|---|---|
| Wins: | _____ | Losses: | _____ |
| KO's: | _____ | KO's: | _____ |
| Subs: | _____ | Subs: | _____ |
| Decisions: | _____ | Decisions: | _____ |

# FIGHT NUMBER 7

## AT MAYHEM AT MIKE'S SPORTS BAR (MAYHEM AT MIKE'S)

**QUESTION 61:** Through 2009, Lyoto Machida and this man were the only non-Americans to hold the UFC's light heavyweight title.
a) Anderson Silva
b) Murilo Bustamante
c) Vitor Belfort
d) Mauricio Rua

**QUESTION 62:** At UFC 46 B.J. Penn took the welterweight belt from Matt Hughes when he subbed him with a rear naked choke in round one. He didn't hold it long because...
a) Hughes won it back in Penn's first title defense
b) Penn was stripped because he signed with K-1
c) Penn was stripped because he signed with PRIDE
d) Penn announced his retirement only to change his mind just two months later

**QUESTION 63:** This famous female fighter's dad was a backup quarterback for the Dallas Cowboys and she was born during a tornado warning.
a) Tara LaRosa
b) Gina Carano
c) Erin Toughill
d) Michelle Waterson

**QUESTION 64:** This man once submitted Olympic Gold Medalist Kenny Monday in just 45 seconds with Sheik Tahnoon Bin Zayed Al Nayhan looking on. The Sheik was so impressed that he asked the man to train him and his team. He did and after one training session Sheik Tahnoon was inspired to start the now famous Abu Dhabi Combat Club's submission wrestling championships.
a) Erik Paulson
b) Greg Jackson
c) Matt Hume
d) B.J. Penn

**QUESTION 65:** After College, Matt Lindland was training and working for a plumbing company when he started giving this young wrestler private lessons and then eventually came on board as the assistant wrestling coach at West Linn High School. He didn't stay long because he was asked to head to Colorado Springs for a pilot program called the Resident Athlete Program. Matt spent four tough years there and it was a very productive and very difficult time for him and his wife Angie and their two young children, James and Robin. He trained, dubbed tapes for USA Wrestling and founded the Foreign Athlete Technical Evaluation System, and even worked at an Ice Skating Rink until well after midnight on most nights. Years later, he was reunited with this wrestler who he'd started giving private lessons to when they came together at what would one day become known as Team Quest.

    a)   Chael Sonnen
    b)   Nate Quarry
    c)   Ed Herman
    d)   Ryan Schultz

**QUESTION 66:** Sticking with Matt Lindland, he earned his nickname "The Law" from his well-known court battle with USA Wrestling and the United States Olympic Committee. After dropping a referee decision at the Greco-Roman Olympic trials to Keith Sieracki (who Matt had beaten numerous times), Matt filed a grievance due to an illegal trip. A rematch was ordered and Matt was given 24 hours notice and had to drop 24 pounds. He still dominated, 9-0. Even then, the USOC didn't want to allow him on the team and even got a "re-arbitration" (ever heard of such a thing?) so he asked the courts to intervene. On the day he was to leave for processing he learned the U.S. Supreme Court sided with him. Even after walking in the opening ceremonies the USOC still tried to take the case to the International Court of Arbitration. The U.S. courts threatened to arrest them for contempt upon return to the States so it didn't happen. After all that, Matt said, "I was so ready. I was done with all that crap. I was there. I was focused. It was not to enjoy the experience ... it was to kick ass!" He took to the mat and earned...

    a)   a Bronze medal
    b)   a Silver medal
    c)   a Gold medal
    d)   a fourth place finish just outside of the podium

**QUESTION 67:** After PRIDE 32 in Las Vegas Mark Coleman, with a distorted face and all, brought his daughters into the ring to console them. He then told them that this man, the one that beat him up, was really a nice guy and introduced them to him.
- a) Mauricio Rua
- b) Antonio Rodrigo Nogueira
- c) Fedor Emelianenko
- d) Mirko Cro Cop Filipovic

**QUESTION 68:** That last one might have been too easy, so what are Mark Coleman's daughters' names?
- a) Tina and Tammy
- b) Mackenzie and Morgan
- c) Melissa and Meredith
- d) Madison and Samantha

**QUESTION 69:** Randy Couture blasted Tim Sylvia with a big right hand just as the fight began. The shot interrupted Mike Goldberg who was in the process of saying, "The first round brought to you by paramount pictures in movies..." What movie and actor did he go on to mention as the crowd was going crazy?
- a) *Ocean's 13* starring George Clooney
- b) *Shooter* starring Mark Wahlberg
- c) *Bangkok Dangerous* starring Nicholas Cage
- d) *Crank* starring Jason Statham

**QUESTION 70:** Mo Lawal was given the nickname "King" from this man when he said, "Once you do what you got to do, you'll be King."

Courtesy of King Mo Lawal.

Mo took the nickname and ran with it. He got a robe custom made and tracked down the crown on dancecheer.net and then wowed the Japanese audiences with his entrances. Who was the man that said, "Once you do what you got to do, you'll be King."

a)  Chris Leben
b)  Jason Miller
c)  Rameau Thierry Sokoudjou
d)  Kami Barzini

## ANSWER KEY FOR FIGHT NUMBER 7
## (MAYHEM AT MIKES)

| QUESTION 61: | C | | QUESTION 66: | B |
|---|---|---|---|---|
| QUESTION 62: | B | | QUESTION 67: | C |
| QUESTION 63: | B | | QUESTION 68: | B |
| QUESTION 64: | C | | QUESTION 69: | B |
| QUESTION 65: | A | | QUESTION 70: | D |

## FIGHT RESULTS

| 10 for 10 | = Win by standing Guillotine choke |
|---|---|
| 9 for 10 | = Win by KO due to knees |
| 8 for 10 | = Unanimous decision victory |
| 7 for 10 | = Split decision victory |
| 6 for 10 | = Split decision loss |
| 5 for 10 | = Unanimous decision loss |
| 4 or fewer | = KO'd by a spinning back fist |

## FIGHT RECORD

Wins: _____       Losses: _____

KO's: _____       KO's: _____

Subs: _____       Subs: _____

Decisions: _____       Decisions: _____

## FIGHT NUMBER 8

## AT ABSOLUTE ADA FIGHTS 5
## (THE RETURN)

**QUESTION 71:** UFC veteran Jorge Rivera served in the U.S. Army as a 19K Armored Cav Scout with A/1-70 in the late 80s early 90s. Almost ten years later he'd found MMA and the middleweight tangled with this much bigger man in a tremendous amateur fight in Rhode Island in October of 1999. Both men went on to have success in the UFC.
   a) Gan McGee
   b) Jeff Monson
   c) Tim Sylvia
   d) Josh Barnett

**QUESTION 72:** Duane "Bang" Ludwig lived up to his nickname when he dropped this man at Ultimate Fight Night 3. The official time was 11 seconds, but the KO actually came only four seconds into the bout.
   a) Jens Pulver
   b) Sam Morgan
   c) Thomas Denny
   d) Jonathan Goulet

**QUESTION 73:** Staying with fast fights, at UFC 6 Oleg Taktarov defeated this man via Guillotine choke in only nine seconds. Many now contend that the fight was a work.
   a) Dave Beneteau
   b) Anthony Macias
   c) Tank Abbott
   d) Marco Ruas

**QUESTION 74:** Mak Takano has trained and advised many MMA stars during his years and is a legend in Japan (he was in *Mr. Baseball* with Tom Selleck). Mak has worked closely with Gesias "JZ" Cavalcante for years and in 2006 saw him win the K-1 HERO'S Middleweight Grand Prix by scoring a split decision over this fighter. Mak said of the fight, "It was a terrible decision because JZ dominated the whole fight and it should have been a unanimous

decision, despite breaking his hand in the first round. He had surgery on it after the victory back in Brazil." The fighter JZ beat was...
- a) Rani Yahya
- b) Caol Uno
- c) Nam Phan
- d) Vitor Ribeiro

QUESTION 75: Staying with Mak and JZ, his name is Gesias Cavalcante, but he's known as JZ Calvan in Japan. Mak explained, "When JZ was first entered into the K-1 MMA HERO'S Tournament, the executives said his name was too long and felt it would be confusing for the Japanese press. So the PR person suggested for us to change it to Calvan to make it easier and catchier for the Japanese people to remember and it would be close to...
- a) Calvin as in Calvin Klein
- b) Calvin as in Calvin and Hobbes
- c) Boxer Calvin Brock who never fought in Japan but was famous for his car commercials
- d) California Van (a Japanese sit-com in the 80s about three college students who lived out of an old Volkswagen Van and called it their "Cal-Van")

QUESTION 76: This man was unable to fight at UFC 99 thanks to pneumonia-like symptoms that exacerbated his asthma. He ended up not fighting the rest of the year and that was okay because he was busy making an untitled horror movie where he plays a gang leader that gets eaten by monsters (sorry for the spoiler).
- a) Heath Herring
- b) Rashad Evans
- c) Quinton Jackson
- d) Matt Serra

QUESTION 77: This man split two decisions with U.S. Army Ranger Tim Kennedy. After the second one he said, "I just play a tough guy on TV, Kennedy is a real American hero." He is definitely right, Tim is a hero. He also loves *Harry Potter*, *Star Wars*, *Star Trek*, *Lord of the Rings*, and other uber-geeky stuff, and plans on leaving the fight

game by 2013 so he can further pursue his military career.
 a) Scott Smith
 b) Jason Miller
 c) Nick Thompson
 d) Dante Rivera

Courtesy of Tim Kennedy.

**QUESTION 78:** Which of the following MMA legends had more wins in PRIDE with 22 overall?
 a) Fedor Emelianenko
 b) Wanderlei Silva
 c) Kazushi Sakuraba
 d) Mirko Cro Cop Filipovic

**QUESTION 79:** Of the aforementioned stars, which one debuted in PRIDE before all the others with a victory at the promotion's second event from the Yokohama Arena on March 15, 1998?
 a) Fedor Emelianenko
 b) Wanderlei Silva
 c) Kazushi Sakuraba
 d) Mirko Cro Cop Filipovic

**QUESTION 80:** Excluding Strikeforce's first fight in MMA back on May 31, 1997 when Brian Johnston subbed John Renfroe, who was

involved in the main event of the promotion's first MMA show in March of 2006?
- a) Frank Shamrock and Cesar Gracie
- b) Alistair Overeem and Vitor Belfort
- c) Tank Abbott and Paul Buentello
- d) Cung Le and Jason Von Flue

## ANSWER KEY FOR FIGHT NUMBER 8
## (THE RETURN)

QUESTION 71:  C              QUESTION 76:  A
QUESTION 72:  D              QUESTION 77:  B
QUESTION 73:  B              QUESTION 78:  B
QUESTION 74:  B              QUESTION 79:  C
QUESTION 75:  A              QUESTION 80:  A

## FIGHT RESULTS

10 for 10      = Win by Superman punch KO
9 for 10       = Win by D'arce choke
8 for 10       = Unanimous decision victory
7 for 10       = Split decision victory
6 for 10       = Split decision loss
5 for 10       = Unanimous decision loss
4 or fewer     = Submitted by flying armbar

## FIGHT RECORD

Wins: _____            Losses: _____

KO's: _____            KO's: _____

Subs: _____            Subs: _____

Decisions: _____       Decisions: _____

## FIGHT NUMBER 9

## THE BOURBON STREET BRAWL FROM MURFREESBORO, TENNESSEE
## (BOURBON STREET BRAWL)

QUESTION 81: This one comes straight from the randomness file. A video surfaced in September of 2009 of UFC announcer Mike Goldberg in a musical adaptation of this popular movie. He is styling some argyle socks and even sings a bit. Only Goldie could pull this off and keep his man card.
   a) *Clueless*
   b) *Legally Blonde*
   c) *Rent*
   d) *Kung Fu Panda*

QUESTION 82: This referee took a tumble during the Tito Ortiz/Lyoto Machida match at UFC 84. He hopped right up though and with a smile on his face.
   a) Yves Lavigne
   b) Steve Mazzagatti
   c) Donnie Jessup
   d) Mario Yamasaki

QUESTION 83: This UFC star's dad was a two-time state wrestling champ in Ohio. He'd lived in Ohio when younger and wrestling was his main sport. "I guess you can say wrestling is in my blood," he says. It was so important to him that he moved back to Ohio and lived with family members for his junior and senior years so he could wrestle at powerhouse all-boys school St. Edward High. "It was the best decision I could have made!" he said.
   a) Mark Coleman
   b) Jorge Gurgel
   c) Gray Maynard
   d) Rich Franklin

QUESTION 84: This man is the only to be involved with the UFC continuously from its inception and as of the beginning of 2010 he's still going strong. In 2009 he got to work in his hometown of

Philadelphia at UFC 101.
   a)   Event coordinator Burt Watson
   b)   Cutman Jacob "Stitch" Duran
   c)   Cutman Leon Tabbs
   d)   Referee Herb Dean

**QUESTION 85:** This man said of Forrest Griffin's book, *Got Fight*, "Forrest Griffin has written a masterpiece. Not since Hemingway has an author stimulated and tantalized the readers' senses through such delicate and colorful prose. This book is destined to become one of the greats, an international bestseller for centuries to come. We should all remove our hats and bow to the genius of this thought-provoking work. Bravo, Griffin, Bravo."
   a)   Mike Pyle
   b)   Randy Couture
   c)   Joe Rogan
   d)   Forrest Griffin

**QUESTION 86:** This man debuted in the UFC at UFC 46 on January 31, 2004 with a decision victory over Karo Parisyan. It would turn out to be the first of many wins.
   a)   Georges St. Pierre
   b)   Matt Hughes
   c)   Josh Thomson
   d)   Chris Lytle

**QUESTION 87:** Also at UFC 46, B.J. Penn won the welterweight belt from Matt Hughes. He then ended up fighting in Japan shortly thereafter, and as Mak Takano, who advised B.J. during his stint in Japan, said, "B.J. wanted to explore the Japanese fight scene ... we put together some interesting fights: Duane Ludwig, Rodrigo Gracie, Renzo Gracie, and even Lyoto Machida." Mak goes on to explain that B.J. requested to fight Lyoto after his original request to fight this man was turned down because of too much of a weight differential.
   a)   Hong Man Choi
   b)   Fedor Emelianenko
   c)   Bob Sapp
   d)   Brock Lesnar (in what would have been his MMA debut)

QUESTION 88: At this gym in San Jose, California you'll find the likes of trainers Dave Camarillo and "Crazy" Bob Cook as well as great fighters: Mike Swick, Jon Fitch, and Josh Koscheck, among others.
a) American Top Team
b) Team Quest
c) The Pit
d) American Kickboxing Academy

QUESTION 89: As the story goes, Kit Cope had been dating Gina Carano and was training at Master Toddy's Muay Thai gym in Las Vegas. Gina showed up and decided she wanted to train and Master Toddy said...
a) "You too pretty to get elbowed."
b) "Ooh baby, you fat."
c) "You look like a lady, but fight like a man."
d) "Sure, just sign here and it will be $99 per month, we're glad to have you."

QUESTION 90: When not in the ring or cage, King Mo likes to chill and listen to music or watch cartoons and Kung Fu flicks. When inside the ring/cage King Mo is not afraid to throw people on their heads as Ryo Kawamura found out the hard way in March of 2009.

Courtesy of King Mo Lawal.

Through six fights and six wins, Mo's win over Kawamura was the only to go to a decision – in large part because of this injury – and later he said, "...I felt like I had enough ring savvy and tools to fight on for the victory."
- a)  a separated shoulder
- b)  a torn ACL
- c)  a broken foot
- d)  a torn hamstring

## ANSWER KEY FOR FIGHT NUMBER 9
## (BOURBON STREET BRAWL)

| | | | | |
|---|---|---|---|---|
| **QUESTION 81:** | B | | **QUESTION 86:** | A |
| **QUESTION 82:** | A | | **QUESTION 87:** | C |
| **QUESTION 83:** | C | | **QUESTION 88:** | D |
| **QUESTION 84:** | C | | **QUESTION 89:** | B |
| **QUESTION 85:** | D | | **QUESTION 90:** | B |

## FIGHT RESULTS

| | |
|---|---|
| 10 for 10 | = Win by armbar Dustin Hazelett style |
| 9 for 10 | = Win by KO from kick to legs |
| 8 for 10 | = Unanimous decision victory |
| 7 for 10 | = Split decision victory |
| 6 for 10 | = Split decision loss |
| 5 for 10 | = Unanimous decision loss |
| 4 or fewer | = KO'd by a short left |

## FIGHT RECORD

| | | | |
|---|---|---|---|
| Wins: | _____ | Losses: | _____ |
| KO's: | _____ | KO's: | _____ |
| Subs: | _____ | Subs: | _____ |
| Decisions: | _____ | Decisions: | _____ |

## Fight Number 10

### Cannes, France Climax Fighting Championships (Down and Dirty)

**Question 91:** This man became Bellator FC's welterweight champ when he TKO'd Omar De La Cruz at Bellator XI on June 12, 2009. The win improved his record to 10-0.
a) Lyman Good
b) Hector Urbina
c) Hector Lombard
d) Igor Gracie

**Question 92:** In *The Official Chuck Norris Fact Book* he talks of training with this legend back in 1982. Norris gained the mount and the man wanted him to punch him. In the book he said, "I can't do that..." He went on, "He insisted, so I drew my hand back timidly like I was going to strike. That's the last thing I remember. When I woke up a few minutes later [he] apologized for choking me so hard."
a) Helio Gracie
b) Rickson Gracie
c) Antonio Inoki
d) Masahiko Kimura

**Question 93:** MMA star Ron Waterman used to be an Art teacher at Greeley West High School, and now he is something else that might seem a little surprising...
a) the President for the Animal Rights Group *M.U.K. (Make up Kills)*
b) a spokesperson for Tony Little's Gazelle Exercise Machine
c) a born again Christian who is also an Ordained Minister
d) the voice of Northern Colorado football on WCOL Radio

**Question 94:** This man should maybe change his nickname to "Rudy" because he never quits. He's had insane come-from-behind

KO's over his buddy Pete Sell, Benji Radach, and Cung Le.
a) Terry Martin
b) Nick Diaz
c) Robbie Lawler
d) Scott Smith

**QUESTION 95:** It was at UFC 83 when Kalib Starnes put on quite a display against this fighter by back peddling for much of the fight and then actually flipping his opponent off after he made fun of Starnes by pretending to run and crossing his arms in front of his face and performing a move he calls "The Rock Hammer."
a) Alan Belcher
b) Nate Quarry
c) Hector Lombard
d) Chris Leben

**QUESTION 96:** This MMA star had a rough upbringing with an abusive father who once placed a gun in his then seven-year-old son's mouth and said, "You aren't worth the bullets." He no doubt overcame the abuse and is an inspiration to many. In 2009 he opened an MMA gym named "Driven" and works to decrease domestic violence.
a) Ken Shamrock
b) Jens Pulver
c) Chuck Liddell
d) Kendall Grove

**QUESTION 97:** The UFC's first branded "UFC gym" held its grand opening in January of 2010. It was quite an affair as there were autograph sessions and seminars all day long with the likes of: Jon Fitch, Mike Swick, Cain Velasquez, Chuck Liddell, Anthony Johnson, Josh Koscheck, and Arianny Celeste. "Our gyms are more than just treadmills and free weights," Dana White said. "We want people to step foot inside a UFC Gym and be a part of an awesome experience." The first taste of the awesome experience was in this city.
a) Las Vegas, Nevada
b) Concord, California
c) Columbus, Ohio
d) Boston, Massachusetts

QUESTION 98: This MMA star was a veteran of PRIDE and also a veteran of Pro Arm Wrestling. Guess it paid off because through 43 fights and a 23-19-1 record he had not been submitted via armbar.
   a)   Valentijn Overeem
   b)   Gary Goodridge
   c)   Patrick Barry
   d)   Igor Vovchanchyn

QUESTION 99: Bruce Buffer worked a little magic to earn an appearance on this popular TV show and it led to him getting a regular spot as the UFC announcer. As he explained it in an article with Dave Doyle at *Yahoo!* Sports, "I called them back afterwards and said, 'Look, I was just on one of the most popular shows in the country as the face of your company. You pretty much have to use me now, don't you?'" The show was...
   a)   *Seinfeld*
   b)   *Murphy's Law*
   c)   *Mad About You*
   d)   *Friends*

QUESTION 100: Sticking with Bruce Buffer, it was at UFC 100 when after a great deal of speculation as to whether he would do it or not, he pulled off this move in the middle of yelling, "Brock-Les-nar!"
   a)   The Buffer 360
   b)   The Bruce Bash
   c)   The Double Dip touch the Lip
   d)   The Bring it around Town

# ANSWER KEY FOR FIGHT NUMBER 10
## (DOWN AND DIRTY)

QUESTION 91:  A          QUESTION 96:  B
QUESTION 92:  A          QUESTION 97:  B
QUESTION 93:  C          QUESTION 98:  B
QUESTION 94:  D          QUESTION 99:  D
QUESTION 95:  B          QUESTION 100: A

## FIGHT RESULTS

10 for 10      = Win by KO from mount
9 for 10       = Win by Anaconda choke
8 for 10       = Unanimous decision victory
7 for 10       = Split decision victory
6 for 10       = Split decision loss
5 for 10       = Unanimous decision loss
4 or fewer     = Subbed by a kneebar

## FIGHT RECORD

Wins:      _____          Losses:    _____

KO's:      _____          KO's:      _____

Subs:      _____          Subs:      _____

Decisions: _____          Decisions: _____

Ranger Up's Tribute to the Great
Strategist Sun Tzu

# Round Three

Ten fights in and you've figured out you've got a knack for ass kicking. Now you've got to start considering all aspects of the fight game. It takes more than just getting in the cage and throwing punches and kicks.

# DEATH GROUND

"IN DIFFICULT GROUND, PRESS ON. On hemmed-in ground, use subterfuge. In death ground, fight."

The quote is from Sun Tzu's *Art of War*. Sun Tzu (544-496 BC) was a Chinese military general and arguably the most influential strategist in the history of China. The *Art of War* has transcended culture and time and is still highly-regarded.

As one legend goes, the King of Wu once asked Sun Tzu if his military strategies would apply to an army of women. Sun Tzu said they would and was put to the test. He divided the 180 concubines into two troops with the King's favorites as the head of each.

Sun Tzu explained the movements and the women said they understood. Then he ordered, "Right turn." The women giggled and did not execute. He explained that if orders were not followed because they are not understood, then the General is to blame, so he repeated the explanation and again gave the order. And again the women giggled.

He then explained that if the orders are clear and understood and still disobeyed, it is the fault of the officers and had the King's two favorite concubines beheaded. The next two took their place and the orders were executed flawlessly thereafter. This is something of an extension of Sun Tzu's death ground strategy. The women were placed in a do-or-die situation.

For Sun Tzu's army, death ground meant taking up a position of which retreat was impossible. There were only two options, victory or death. But as can be seen by the above quote, there was more to the strategy, and this is where modern Mixed Martial Artists come in.

The difficult ground can be found in the gym. Here a man must press on, push forward despite the pain and bodily punishment associated with persistent training.

Hemmed-in ground can be found as the fight nears, when the opponents are face to face. Here, a fighter can use subterfuge. Words and actions can be employed in a way that can hide one's true intentions or disrupt the opponent's confidence.

Then there is the modern sport fighter's figurative death ground. It is a patch of canvas that transforms once the cage door closes and the pin is slid into place. And when on death ground there is only one thing to do ... *fight!*

## FIGHT NUMBER 11

## ROVANIEMI, FINLAND'S ARCTIC FIGHTS (DAMN IT'S COLD UP HERE!)

**QUESTION 101:** This fight was named *Fighters Only* World Mixed Martial Arts Awards 2009 Fight of the Year, and it was well-deserved, with the first minute or so an all out slobber knocker.
- a)   Mike Brown vs. Urijah Faber
- b)   Diego Sanchez vs. Clay Guida
- c)   Randy Couture vs. Antonio Rodrigo Nogueira
- d)   Rich Franklin vs. Wanderlei Silva

**QUESTION 102:** The Kimbo Slice slayer Seth Petruzelli held a solid 11-4 record through 15 fights. He was also a contestant on *The Ultimate Fighter* season two and just before he dropped Kimbo he started thinking of making money outside of fighting when he...
- a)   began an Internet reality TV show that follows him rollerblading along Florida's beaches and interacting with unsuspecting tourists while wearing nothing but a thong.
- b)   opened a Smoothie King that was so successful he had plans to open another.
- c)   began selling high-end women's shoes designed by his wife Leslie.
- d)   became a celebrity spokesman for Buffalo Wild Wings after eating 57 Blazin' wings in only 11 minutes.

**QUESTION 103:** This man goes by the nickname "Nasty" and fought in UFC 1 where he lost to Kevin Rosier. Heading into the event he bumped into Ken Shamrock. "I saw Ken Shamrock. He was all bundled up and I couldn't see his physique or anything. He said, 'My name's Ken Shamrock.' I said, 'So f-***** what? I'm going to kick your f-***** ass. You're going to leave here in a body bag.' And that's how I was to everybody. I remember Ken taking off his shirt a couple days later and saw how buff and yoked he was. I said, 'Oh, s-**! This guy would've twisted me up!' My heart came through my

throat."
a)   Trent Jenkins
b)   Teila Tuli
c)   Zane Frazier
d)   Gerard Gordeau

QUESTION 104: Referee Dan Miragliotta really did his part to rough up this fighter as he took on Dan Hardy at UFC 89. First he knocked the man right out of the air as he tried a flying knee at the bell, and then Miragliotta pushed this fighter to the canvas late in the third when he illegally kneed Hardy while he was on the ground.
a)   Akihiro Gono
b)   Marcus Davis
c)   Mike Swick
d)   Rory Markham

QUESTION 105: Chael Sonnen is more than just a fighter. Starting in 2002 he began operating this MMA organization (the only sanctioned by the State Athletic Commission for a time) and in 2003 he put on an event to help raise funds for fellow fighter Josh Haynes' young son who was battling a brain tumor. Evan Tanner fought on the *Fighting Against Cancer* card and the proceeds helped the Haynes family as Thor beat the disease. Chael's promotion has also helped 13 athletes make their way to the UFC and its name is…
a)   Absolute Submission Fighting
b)   Full Contact Fighting Federation
c)   Sportfight
d)   Xtreme Ultimate Combat

QUESTION 106: It was just mentioned that Chael was more than just a fighter. He is more than just a promoter too. His father was a builder and developer, his parents owned a Century 21, and his sister is a real estate attorney. He got into fixing homes up and selling them, then merged into representing others. Now, despite his tremendous success as a professional fighter, Chael is still a real estate agent for this company…
a)   Century 21, Gresham Office
b)   Joseph Albert Wapner and Associates of Portland, Oregon
c)   The Oregon Real Estate Agency Group of Bend, Oregon
d)   John L. Scott, West Linn-Cascade Summit Office

QUESTION **107**: Australian Michael Schiavello is an international sports presenter and known as The Voice. He has done numerous martial arts events, including: K-1, DREAM, Sengoku and others. He is known for his hilarious one-liners, so which one did he *NOT* say?
- a)  "He has no chance of winning this, unless maybe a safe falls on his opponents head!"
- b)  On Hong Man Choi, "He's so tall when he walks past the zoo giraffes are attracted to him."
- c)  "I tell you now he will win this fight. If he doesn't you can pinch my cheeks and call me buttercup while I salsa dance to reggae music."
- d)  "He's so short he could milk a cow standing up. You know he went to Tokyo Disneyland last week and they wouldn't let him on any of the rides."

QUESTION **108**: Sticking with the hilarity of The Voice, after this fighter's third head kick KO in a row, this one came at the expense of Myeon Ho Bae at DREAM 12, Schiavello yelled, "We can do no wrong you and I, me commentating and you fighting. Go sunshine! You've done it again."
- a)  Marius Zaromskis
- b)  Mirko Cro Cop Filipovic
- c)  Gilbert Yvel
- d)  Alistair Overeem

QUESTION **109**: In his book, this UFC star admits to wetting the bed until the eighth grade (double dog dare you to make fun of him). It wasn't until the seventh grade when he started peeing blood that the doctors figured out he had an enlarged bladder. He obviously overcame it and went on to become a UFC champ and one of the most popular MMA figures in the history of the sport.
- a)  Randy Couture
- b)  Tito Ortiz
- c)  Matt Hughes
- d)  Chuck Liddell

QUESTION **110**: This fighter was born in France and lived there until he was nine. He then lived in the Canary Islands and Vancouver B.C. and he can speak French, English, Spanish, and Portuguese. His parents are multi-lingual too, but they haven't fought in as many places. Through 45 fights and a 32-12-1 record this man has fought in the U.S., Japan, England, Canada, South Korea, Ireland, and Russia.

   a) Cheick Kongo
   b) Jess Liaudin
   c) Denis Kang
   d) Pierre Guillet

## ANSWER KEY FOR FIGHT NUMBER 11
## (DAMN IT'S COLD UP HERE!)

| | |
|---|---|
| QUESTION 101: B | QUESTION 106: D |
| QUESTION 102: B | QUESTION 107: C |
| QUESTION 103: C | QUESTION 108: A |
| QUESTION 104: A | QUESTION 109: A |
| QUESTION 105: B | QUESTION 110: C |

## FIGHT RESULTS

| | |
|---|---|
| 10 for 10 | = Win by double flying knee KO |
| 9 for 10 | = Win by flying armbar |
| 8 for 10 | = Unanimous decision victory |
| 7 for 10 | = Split decision victory |
| 6 for 10 | = Split decision loss |
| 5 for 10 | = Unanimous decision loss |
| 4 or fewer | = Subbed by broken arm due to hammerlock |

## FIGHT RECORD

| Wins: _____ | Losses: _____ |
|---|---|
| KO's: _____ | KO's: _____ |
| Subs: _____ | Subs: _____ |
| Decisions: _____ | Decisions: _____ |

## FIGHT NUMBER 12

### AT THE LAZY E ARENA IN GUTHRIE, OKLAHOMA
### (BATTLE AMONGST THE CATTLE)

**QUESTION 111:** This Philadelphia Phillies star is friends with B.J. Penn and a big MMA fan. At UFC 101 Dana White wore his jersey number during the weigh in.
   a) Jimmy Rollins
   b) Ryan Howard
   c) Brad Lidge
   d) Shane Victorino

**QUESTION 112:** ESPN photographer Martin McNeil took an extremely powerful photo of Joe Stevenson after he lost to this fighter at UFC 80.

Joe Stevenson – courtesy of Martin McNeil.

Almost two years later at UFC 105, Martin got to visit with Joe about it and said, "I saw this moment as an ideal (yet awkward) time to thank him for the infamous shot. Turns out I had nothing to worry about." Joe responded, "You know, that moment, it's kind of

a bad memory but it's a memory all the same – a bit like a messy divorce. I'm glad that something positive came out of it though."
   a) Sean Sherk
   b) B.J. Penn
   c) Diego Sanchez
   d) Kenny Florian

QUESTION 113: In this fight at PRIDE 21, the combatants went crazy for six minutes and ten seconds as they punched each other at a breakneck pace until one of them finally scored a TKO. The fight was so exciting that it was re-enacted for the Japanese movie *Nagurimono*.
   a) Don Frye vs. Yoshihiro Takayama
   b) Ken Shamrock vs. Kazuyuki Fujita
   c) Kazushi Sakuraba vs. Carlos Newton
   d) Anderson Silva vs. Alex Stiebling

QUESTION 114: This fighter – nicknamed "The Barncat" – was cut from the UFC despite a 3-3 record with the promotion after losing a split decision at UFC 101 against John Howard.
   a) Dustin Hazelett
   b) Ryan Madigan
   c) Tamdan McCrory
   d) Chris Wilson

QUESTION 115: UFC President Dana White was on vacation when he saw this man fight Drew Fickett. White was scouting Fickett for TUF season one, but after the fight he asked Drew's opponent, who he called "pudgy" at around 180 pounds, to be on the show instead.
   a) Kenny Florian
   b) Josh Koscheck
   c) Diego Sanchez
   d) Alexis Karalexis

QUESTION 116: Keeping with guys who almost made it on the first season of *The Ultimate Fighter*, this man was at the airport with his bags already on the plane when he got the call not to get on the flight. Seems there was a last minute change and he did not appear

on the show.
a)  Karo Parisyan
b)  Jon Fitch
c)  Joe Lauzon
d)  Sam Stout

QUESTION 117: David Gardner made a big time boo-boo when he decided to yell, "Hello Japan," and wave to the crowd while this man was on his back at DREAM 7. His opponent took advantage and sunk in a rear naked choke to end the fight.
a)  Tatsuya Kawajiri
b)  Joe Warren
c)  Yoshiro Maeda
d)  Shinya Aoki

QUESTION 118: This Louisianan started training after joining the Navy at the age of 18 and was a contestant on *The Ultimate Fighter* season 7. Through 15 fights he was 12-3 overall and 3-1 in the UFC.
a)  Jesse Taylor
b)  Matt Brown
c)  Tim Credeur
d)  Matt Riddle

QUESTION 119: This man had his left arm broke early in the first round against Edson "Paredao" Silva (Paredao translates to thick wall in Portuguese) in Brazil in 2003. Instead of tapping, he promptly KO'd Paredao with a right. He then went to a Brazilian hospital where he talked of a burly guy in overalls putting the cast on. Upon returning to the States he learned the break was severe enough to garner surgery and a steel plate, but he didn't have the money so now he has a knot on his arm.
a)  Chuck Liddell
b)  Forrest Griffin
c)  Mac Danzig
d)  Jamie Varner

QUESTION 120: This MMA star fought in the U.S. just four times through 33 fights. Two of these four came in 2009 when the man was really introduced to U.S. fans, even making an appearance on CBS. He won both of them, but of course it was expected because he

wins pretty much all of his fights.
  a)   Fedor Emelianenko
  b)   Gegard Mousasi
  c)   Shinya Aoki
  d)   Paulo Filho

# ANSWER KEY FOR FIGHT NUMBER 12
## (BATTLE AMONGST THE CATTLE)

QUESTION 111: D          QUESTION 116: B
QUESTION 112: B          QUESTION 117: D
QUESTION 113: A          QUESTION 118: C
QUESTION 114: C          QUESTION 119: B
QUESTION 115: A          QUESTION 120: A

## FIGHT RESULTS

| | |
|---|---|
| 10 for 10 | = Win by inverted triangle/Kimura |
| 9 for 10 | = Win by left hook |
| 8 for 10 | = Unanimous decision victory |
| 7 for 10 | = Split decision victory |
| 6 for 10 | = Split decision loss |
| 5 for 10 | = Unanimous decision loss |
| 4 or fewer | = Subbed by broken arm due to hammerlock – *again!* |

## FIGHT RECORD

Wins: _____          Losses: _____

KO's: _____          KO's: _____

Subs: _____          Subs: _____

Decisions: _____          Decisions: _____

## FIGHT NUMBER 13

## AT THE CLEVELAND ARENA
## (ROCK & RUMBLE 4)

**QUESTION 121:** Chris Leben had a busy year in 2006. He fought a UFC record (excluding tournaments) five times on the year and went 3-2. He said of the stretch, "You know it really wasn't anything because as an amateur and before I got into the UFC I was fairly active, fighting maybe seven or eight times a year. It was great to really shotgun me into the mainstream in the UFC and getting respected as a legitimate 185 pounder." His victories came against Jorge Rivera, Luigi Fioravanti and this man at UFC Fight Night 6.
   a)   Jason Thacker
   b)   Jorge Santiago
   c)   Alessio Sakara
   d)   Terry Martin

Courtesy of Chris Leben.

**QUESTION 122:** Quinton "Rampage" Jackson has three sons: D'Angelo, Raja, and Elijah, and their middle names are Rampage. He

also has one daughter, Nakia, and her middle name is…
a) Rampage
b) Pageina
c) Page
d) Quinton

QUESTION 123: At PRIDE 22 Anderson Silva danced his way to the ring to this song.
a) Cypress Hill's *Insane in the Membrane*
b) Michael Jackson's *Don't Stop Until You Get Enough*
c) Phil Collins' *I Can Feel it Coming in the Air*
d) A-Ha's *Take on Me*

QUESTION 124: After Anderson wowed the crowd with his entrance he scored a decision over this opponent.
a) Alexander Otsuka
b) Alex Stiebling
c) Jeremy Horn
d) Carlos Newton

QUESTION 125: A few fights after Anderson Silva's, Quinton Jackson squared off with Igor Vovchanchyn. During the stare down he handed Igor a note that was reportedly from his mom and read, *Please don't hurt my son.* How did the fight between Igor and Quinton end?
a) Igor brutally KO'd Jackson and then apologized to his mother
b) Jackson's mom need not worry, he KO'd Igor in the first round
c) the fight went to a decision with Jackson claiming the victory and Igor, angry about the results, ripped up the note
d) coincidentally (considering the note and all) Igor submitted in the first round because his ribs/side was injured after a Jackson punch

QUESTION 126: Matt Lindland compiled an impressive 21-7 record overall and was 9-3 in the UFC through 2009. He jumped into MMA with Dan Henderson and Randy Couture and the three of them invented the Dirty Boxing style of fighting (Matt even has a great book out, *Dirty Boxing for Mixed Martial Arts*). They began training together in this unique place that was Matt's prior business before his partner ripped him off, and believe it or not, Team Quest is still in the same location, albeit it's gone through hundreds of thousands of dollars of upgrades.

    a)   a health club
    b)   in the auto shop of Matt Lindland's USA auto sales
    c)   a Daylight Donuts
    d)   a warehouse for Matt's moving company

**QUESTION 127:** Rashad Evans earned his Brazilian Jiu Jitsu black belt from this man on January 2, 2010, the day he beat Thiago Silva at UFC 108. Despite the accomplishment, Rashad did not go for a submission in the fight keeping his total number of sub attempts in the UFC at zero.

    a)   Lloyd Irvin
    b)   Rolles Gracie
    c)   Cesar Gracie
    d)   Pedro Sauer

**QUESTION 128:** Frank Shamrock beat Tito Ortiz in a thrilling middleweight championship fight at UFC 22 and then announced his retirement in the cage. He did so because...

    a)   he'd decided to pursue other interests and opened a health spa in San Jose, California that failed a year later, hence his return to fighting in a K-1 event
    b)   he was frustrated with the recent advent of more rules and five minute rounds and wanted to fight in organizations that did not have such rules
    c)   PRIDE offered him an unprecedented one million dollars to fight in its promotion and he accepted, but the deal fell through and Frank never did fight for PRIDE
    d)   the cash-strapped UFC could not pay him the agreed-upon amount so a deal was made that if he should win he would publicly announce his retirement and that he was vacating the title and the UFC would release claims on him

**QUESTION 129:** These brothers were the first to appear on the

same UFC card.
   a)   Frank and Ken Shamrock
   b)   Joe and Dan Lauzon
   c)   Jim and Dan Miller
   d)   Cole and Micah Miller

QUESTION 130: This man got interested in fighting, like so many others, by watching old UFC tapes. After training in Hapkido and BJJ he felt bold enough to give it a shot and his trainer at the time, Marcus Soares, got him his first fight in 1998. He won, but was just 7-7 after 14 fights. Then he went on a tear by going a remarkable 21-0-1 over his next 22 fights, including wins over Andrei Semenov, Mark Weir, Amir Suloev, and Murilo Rua and back-to-back KO's in only 27 seconds!
   a)   Igor Vovchanchyn
   b)   Quinton Jackson
   c)   Denis Kang
   d)   Dennis Hallman

## ANSWER KEY FOR FIGHT NUMBER 13
### (ROCK & RUMBLE 4)

QUESTION 121: B        QUESTION 126: B
QUESTION 122: C        QUESTION 127: B
QUESTION 123: B        QUESTION 128: D
QUESTION 124: A        QUESTION 129: B
QUESTION 125: D        QUESTION 130: C

## FIGHT RESULTS

10 for 10      = KO win via ground and pound
9 for 10       = Win by heel hook
8 for 10       = Unanimous decision victory
7 for 10       = Split decision victory
6 for 10       = Split decision loss
5 for 10       = Unanimous decision loss
4 or fewer     = KO'd by superman punch

## FIGHT RECORD

Wins: _____          Losses: _____

KO's: _____          KO's: _____

Subs: _____          Subs: _____

Decisions: _____     Decisions: _____

# FIGHT NUMBER 14

## AT THE HERSHEY, PENNSYLVANIA CIVIC CENTER (SUGAR AND SPICE)

QUESTION 131: Mackens Semerzier came out of seemingly nowhere to become the first man to submit Jiu Jitsu black belt Wagnney Fabiano at WEC 43 in October of 2009. Many called the win the upset of the year. Mackens gives much of the credit for his success to...
   a)   his three big brothers who used to beat the crap out of him almost every day.
   b)   his days of getting in an estimated 150 street fights in Miami and he jokes that he should have videoed them like Kimbo
   c)   hours and hours of watching Gracie Jiu Jitsu instructional videos
   d)   the Marine Corp Martial Arts Program, Mackens was a U.S. Marine for eight years

QUESTION 132: Going back to Mackens' triangle submission of Wagnney Fabiano, this WEC star was in his corner and had told him before the bout that if he cinched the triangle he should add a few elbows to bloody Fabiano before he escaped (figuring like everybody else that there was no way Mackens could submit him). Mackens did deliver some elbows, but Fabiano didn't escape and the end came at 2:14 of round one. The man in Mackens' corner was...
   a)   Miguel Torres
   b)   Brian Bowles
   c)   Jamie Varner
   d)   Marcus Hicks

QUESTION 133: This UFC star appeared on the popular cable network G4TV's most popular show "Attack of the Show" in 2009 to promote the sequel to the 2008 Video Game of the Year, Left4Dead. Valve Software, the creators of Left4Dead 2 used his face as the model for one of the zombie characters in the new

version.
- a) Clay Guida
- b) Rich Franklin
- c) Nate Quarry
- d) Keith Jardine

**QUESTION 134:** Sticking with the zombie UFC fighter. He also jokingly talked of his desire to create a comic book that harkened back to the days when the sport was still in its infancy and purely underground, but with a twist. His vision? "Zombie Cagefighting" pitting cagefighters against zombies. "Rules for humans, no biting. For zombies ... mostly biting." The setting for where the Zombie Cagefights take place was drawn from his experience surrounding his first fight, which took place in...
- a) a field behind a bar
- b) a ring set up on a beach in Northern California
- c) a Fraternity house
- d) a warehouse

**QUESTION 135:** Patrick Cote made his UFC debut on only four days notice against Tito Ortiz in the featured fight of this event. Cote replaced an injured Guy Mezger and said of the fight, "It was a crazy start for me in the UFC, but at the same time in was perfect. I was a nobody and had nothing to lose. It was a win-win situation. I wasn't nervous at all." Cote lost a decision, but impressed many with his game effort.
- a) UFC 47
- b) UFC 50
- c) Ultimate Fight Night
- d) UFC 67

**QUESTION 136:** Staying with Patrick Cote, he fought Anderson Silva for the middleweight belt at UFC 90 and suffered a freak knee injury in round three. It was actually in round two when he felt his ACL go but continued because it was for the belt. In the third, pretty much everything else in his knee blew out. The injury meant a ton of recovery time and rehabilitation to strengthen the knee. Hopefully during 2009 he got to spend some time on the golf course and time with his golden retriever named Tito, because as a

kid Patrick wanted to...
   a)  be a dog trainer and take his dogs to the Westminster Dog Show
   b)  be a veterinarian
   c)  be a professional golfer
   d)  build a nine-hole golf course on land owned by his family

QUESTION 137: Mike Goldberg's first UFC event was Ultimate Japan 1 back in December of 1997 and his one-hundredth event was UFC 91 in November of 2008. This fighter actually appeared on both cards, winning in 1997 and losing in 2008.
   a)  Joe Stevenson
   b)  Vitor Belfort
   c)  Jorge Gurgel
   d)  Randy Couture

QUESTION 138: This fighter made his return to the UFC Octagon after he called in to the MMA Junkie radio show upon learning that Dana White would be on it. "At first Dana thought I was some British guy calling in to ask a question," he said. "Then he figured out that it was me and was like 'Dude, I need you back, call me.' I got a hold of him later that day and now look, I'm back." He returned on the UFN 20 card and scored a TKO victory.
   a)  Rory MacDonald
   b)  Gerald Harris
   c)  Jesse Lennox
   d)  Kyle Bradley

QUESTION 139: This exciting fighter claimed a UFC record five fight of the night awards in his first eight UFC bouts. And to top it off he threw in a submission of the night. Talk about making some coin.
   a)  Tyson Griffin
   b)  Forrest Griffin
   c)  Chris Lytle
   d)  Paul Taylor

QUESTION 140: This man took a fight against Kid Yamamoto back in 2007 and lost a decision. "He wanted to fight and wanted the challenge," said Mak Takano, who works closely with him. "He lost in a close decision but the experience to fight on a big stage was huge and it helped him to prepare for his dream, the DREAM

Featherweight Tournament." This fighter went on to win that tournament in 2009.
    a)  Joe Warren
    b)  Hiroyuki Takaya
    c)  Yoshiro Maeda
    d)  Bibiano Fernandes

# ANSWER KEY FOR FIGHT NUMBER 14
## (SUGAR AND SPICE)

QUESTION 131: D      QUESTION 136: C
QUESTION 132: A      QUESTION 137: D
QUESTION 133: C      QUESTION 138: B
QUESTION 134: D      QUESTION 139: A
QUESTION 135: B      QUESTION 140: D

## FIGHT RESULTS

10 for 10      = KO win by brutal overhand right
9 for 10       = Win via Guillotine
8 for 10       = Unanimous decision victory
7 for 10       = Split decision victory
6 for 10       = Split decision loss
5 for 10       = Unanimous decision loss
4 or fewer     = Submitted by Anaconda choke

## FIGHT RECORD

Wins:        _____        Losses:       _____

KO's:        _____        KO's:         _____

Subs:        _____        Subs:         _____

Decisions:   _____        Decisions:    _____

## FIGHT NUMBER 15

## THE CORN PALACE IN MITCHELL, NORTH DAKOTA (CARNAGE AT THE CORN)

**QUESTION 141:** This WEC lightweight champ got a rather enjoyable rehab assignment after breaking his hand against Donald Cerrone in January 2009. The doctor ordered him to play video games (thought we were going a different route?). Unfortunately he had loaned his Xbox to friend Ryan Bader. He got it back in time for the release of Call of Duty: Modern Warfare 2 and said, "I've been on that non-stop pretty much."
   a)   Urijah Faber
   b)   Ben Henderson
   c)   Jamie Varner
   d)   Rob McCullough

**QUESTION 142:** At UFC 2 Fred Ettish was a late replacement for this man who was injured in an earlier bout. He barely had time to warm up before he found himself in the Octagon.
   a)   Jason Delucia
   b)   Scott Baker
   c)   Patrick Smith
   d)   Frank Hamaker

**QUESTION 143:** Fred Ettish fought this man at UFC 2 and lost in pretty brutal fashion. The fight turned Ettish into the butt of jokes for years to come and many called him the "Fetal Fighter" because of his performance.
   a)   Johnny Rhodes
   b)   Scott Morris
   c)   Royce Gracie
   d)   Remco Pardoel

**QUESTION 144:** Despite the setback at UFC 2, Ettish continued to train and years later, thanks to his friend Brock Larson, Ettish was able to step back in the cage once again. It wasn't in the UFC, but at Larson's Cagefighting Xtreme where Ettish looked for redemption. In an interview at Sherdog he'd said, "I have a lot of ghosts and demons that have not been put to rest, and I've come to the conclusion that the only way to do this is to get back in there and actually do my best and represent in a way I can be proud of. I guess I don't want to die at 0-1." He won't die 0-1 because he beat Kyle Fletcher in almost the same length of time it took him to lose at UFC 2. The story gets even better when you consider Ettish's age at the time of his second fight. How old was he?

a)  45
b)  49
c)  53
d)  60

**QUESTION 145:** This man was Dana White's first (and only) Jiu Jitsu coach and he also was the first man to have a fight in the UFC stopped in the third round. At UFC 22 he stopped Lowell Anderson at 14 seconds of round three.

a)  Jeremy Horn
b)  Jorge Gurgel
c)  Dave Camarillo
d)  John Lewis

**QUESTION 146:** Rich Clementi spent three years in Bosnia as a Navy Seabee and was a reservist called to duty after 9/11. He's also had over 50 MMA fights, runs Rich Clementi's Gladiators Academy, and in 2006 he started the MMA promotion No Love Entertainment. The dude has done a lot of stuff and ironically, "No Love" found love in his second wife Amanda and they have also opened this unique type of business together.

a)  a video store
b)  an Italian restaurant (the only in Slidell, Louisiana)
c)  a Tanning Salon
d)  a rock climbing school

**QUESTION 147:** Amazingly, Chris Leben fought on the first six UFC Fight Nights and fared well by putting together this impressive record. When talking of these fights he said, "I was on a roll! I think the UFC was really riding the wave as well, putting me in whenever they could. Also, I'm an exciting fighter. People like to watch me

fight, I sell tickets. That's the bottom line." His record was ... ?
- a)   4-2
- b)   5-1
- c)   6-0
- d)   4-1-1

Courtesy of Chris Leben.

**QUESTION 148:** The last question (or should I say one of the possible answers) reminded me; back in 2001 future UFC fighter Drew Fickett was forced to face this TV judge because he was being sued for damaging the top of a woman's car at a party at the University of Arizona. He had to pay $2,000 to Michelle Mergner and wasn't too fired up about it, but this Judge didn't care.
- a)   Judge Judy
- b)   Judge Joe Brown
- c)   Judge Alex
- d)   Judge Marilyn Milian

**QUESTION 149:** This man became the WEC's first lightweight champ when he defeated Olaf Alfonso at WEC 10 on May 21, 2004. He then vacated the title because he left the WEC and went on to become the champ in another high-profile organization,

Strikeforce.
   a)  Gilbert Melendez
   b)  Josh Thomson
   c)  Clay Guida
   d)  Hermes Franca

**QUESTION 150:** Exactly five months after Olaf Alfonso got the crack at the WEC belt, he got another try at WEC 12, but was once again beat by this man who went on to defend the belt twice. A couple years later he appeared on the fifth season of *The Ultimate Fighter* and it was not so good.
   a)  Sam Wells
   b)  Gabe Ruediger
   c)  Hermes Franca
   d)  Nate Diaz

## ANSWER KEY FOR FIGHT NUMBER 15
### (CARNAGE AT THE CORN)

QUESTION 141: C

QUESTION 142: D

QUESTION 143: A

QUESTION 144: C

QUESTION 145: D

QUESTION 146: C

QUESTION 147: B

QUESTION 148: A

QUESTION 149: A

QUESTION 150: B

## FIGHT RESULTS

| | |
|---|---|
| 10 for 10 | = Submission win via triangle/armbar |
| 9 for 10 | = KO via knee from the clinch |
| 8 for 10 | = Unanimous decision victory |
| 7 for 10 | = Split decision victory |
| 6 for 10 | = Split decision loss |
| 5 for 10 | = Unanimous decision loss |
| 4 or fewer | = KO'd by double flying knee |

## FIGHT RECORD

Wins: _____          Losses: _____

KO's: _____          KO's: _____

Subs: _____          Subs: _____

Decisions: _____          Decisions: _____

Ranger Up's Tribute to the Incomparable
Samurai Miyamoto Musashi

# Round Four

It's time to make a run. Your training is on the spot, your skills have improved, you're hungry, and you want to be a champion.

# MUSASHI SAMURAI

IMAGINE THAT YOU ARE 13 YEARS OLD and you've challenged a grown man to a fight. Your uncle does his best to call it off, but the man insists that the only way you can restore his honor is by apologizing during the scheduled time of the dual.

You and your uncle arrive and he begins apologizing on your behalf. You glare at the swordsman as he stands with a smug look on his face and companion sword in his hand. Your own hands squeeze your six-foot quarterstaff. You scream a challenge to the man even as your uncle is trying to apologize. Then you attack.

The man uses his Wakizashi and you dodge the sword and throw him to the ground. Then you blast him in the face and continue beating him until he is motionless.

This is how Miyamoto Musashi's first dual went down, and it was the first of many. Three years later he left his village and traveled and fought. Over the years he defeated numerous worthy opponents and became known for his strategy of using both his long sword and companion sword. He once defeated up to 30 attackers with this technique as he killed so swiftly that many of the men lost their nerve.

Then on April 13, 1612 he reached the tiny island of Funajima well after the scheduled time of his dual with Sasaki Kojiro, the only man regarded as his equal. As the story goes (one of many) Kojiro was furious with the late arrival and then Musashi taunted him. Along the way he fashioned an oversized bokken, or wooden sword, from an oar. Kojiro attacked using his famous swallow cut technique, but Musashi's sword struck Kojiro first. The man fell and Musashi delivered a blow to the ribs that punctured his lung. He then returned to his boat and rode the out-going tide away from the island.

Of the numerous accounts, one thing seems certain in most. Musashi used various tactics to give himself an advantage. Through the years he had become a masterful strategist and toward the end of his life he wrote of his strategies during confrontation and his warrior philosophy.

Musashi's *The Book of Five Rings* is filled with timeless principles that are still used today in all walks of life, including modern Mixed Martial Arts. He writes of the importance of training, of remaining calm and balanced in preparation and during combat, of the importance of becoming adept in more than just one area, and of the need to learn how to perceive that which you cannot quite comprehend.

These principles are a must for success in modern sport fighting. When a man gains competence in each area he is hard to beat, and with any level of mastery in each of the areas he might even become unbeatable, like the Samurai Miyamoto Musashi.

## FIGHT NUMBER 16

## CAGE RAGE AT THE WEMBLEY ARENA
## (FEEL THE PAIN)

**QUESTION 151:** This event in October of 1997 introduced us to a fan that has now become known as the legendary "Just Bleed" guy.
   a) UFC 1 The Beginning
   b) UFC 8 David vs. Goliath
   c) UFC 15 Collision Course
   d) UFC 17 Redemption

**QUESTION 152:** At the aforementioned "Just Bleed" guy event, this man, a practitioner of RIP, entered the Octagon with a 30-0 record in Army bear pitfights but it only took Mark Kerr one knee and just under 20 seconds to end his night.
   a) Dwayne Cason
   b) Moti Horenstein
   c) Dan Bobish
   d) Greg Stott

**QUESTION 153:** Sticking with the "Just Bleed" guy (come on he's an icon), he may not even know he is an Internet legend because...
   a) he is reportedly currently serving time in a Mississippi prison for receiving stolen property
   b) he was beaten up badly in a bar fight and suffered from amnesia and never fully recovered
   c) amazingly he is a zoologist and has spent the last five years (since 2005) studying the water movement and temperature underneath the ice in Antarctica as it is theorized that this may affect global warming
   d) he simply cannot figure out how to use the Internet

**QUESTION 154:** If you know this you might be a "Just Bleed" guy stalker. His real name is
   a) Doug Norville
   b) James Ladner
   c) Terry Stidham
   d) Bobby Whitaker

QUESTION 155: Sticking with the "Just Bleed" guy (again, he is a symbol of the early UFC's so screw off if you're tired of him), it was at UFC 100 when this fighter offered up a nice tribute to him by painting his forehead with "UFC" and his chest with "Just Bleed" during the UFC 100 weigh in.
- a) Tom Lawlor
- b) Frank Mir
- c) Alan Belcher
- d) Stephan Bonnar

QUESTION 156: Also at UFC 100, Tom Lawlor had a unique entrance to *Who Let the Dogs Out* and walked to the Octagon with this fighter on a leash with a bone in his mouth. At one point the leashed fighter even stopped to hike his leg and the whole thing was even more impressive considering he was wearing flip-flops.
- a) Jason Miller
- b) Seth Petruzelli
- c) Dan Quinn
- d) Tank Abbott

QUESTION 157: In an interview at Cage Potato, Tom Lawlor talked of the crazy UFC 100 entrance and said, "...It would have been funny, maybe, but once you add in the element of, there's a man, a grown man, acting like a dog and, wait a minute, he's got a bone in his mouth, he drops it out of his mouth, then picks it up off the dirty Vegas floor and puts it right back in his mouth. That changes things. It ups the ante and makes things a bit more serious, and more spectacular at the same time." The entrance idea came about because Lawlor was fighting C.B. Dollaway. Dollaway's nickname is...
- a) The Big Dog
- b) The Pitbull
- c) The Doberman
- d) The Dog Pound

QUESTION 158: In an interview at Five Knuckles, Tim Credeur talked of how his desire to get into combat sports came from his dad and the guys at his dad's restaurant who would watch boxing on Sunday nights. "I'd see these guys at the restaurant all the time leading normal lives, with all the same problems everybody else has, but for that hour or two we were watching fights ... they were just out of their minds. I remember as a kid thinking, how incredible would it be to give people that kind of excitement and be a part of something like that." He probably gave those very same guys that excitement during his last fight of 2009 against this man. Tim dropped a really close decision, but it was no doubt one of the best fights of the year.

   a)   Nick Catone
   b)   Nate Loughran
   c)   Chael Sonnen
   d)   Nate Quarry

Courtesy of Tim Credeur.

**QUESTION 159:** In his book *Made in America,* Matt Hughes talks of how after he beat Royce Gracie at UFC 60 this woman approached him and said, "I lost a bet and I was wondering if you would sign my breast."

   a)   Cindy Crawford
   b)   Laura Prepon
   c)   Paris Hilton
   d)   Mandy Moore

QUESTION 160: Also from his book, a day after the "breast signing" Matt Hughes and his family and this MMA star made a trip to Disneyland. Talk about an odd group on the Tea Cup ride!
   a)   Tito Ortiz
   b)   Mike Swick
   c)   Chuck Liddell
   d)   Tim Sylvia

## ANSWER KEY FOR FIGHT NUMBER 16
## (FEEL THE PAIN)

QUESTION 151: C

QUESTION 152: D

QUESTION 153: A

QUESTION 154: B

QUESTION 155: A

QUESTION 156: B

QUESTION 157: C

QUESTION 158: D

QUESTION 159: A

QUESTION 160: C

## FIGHT RESULTS

| | |
|---|---|
| 10 for 10 | = KO from ground and pound back mount |
| 9 for 10 | = Sub via filthy Guillotine choke |
| 8 for 10 | = Unanimous decision victory |
| 7 for 10 | = Split decision victory |
| 6 for 10 | = Split decision loss |
| 5 for 10 | = Unanimous decision loss |
| 4 or fewer | = Subbed by neck crank |

## FIGHT RECORD

Wins:        _____        Losses:        _____

KO's:        _____        KO's:        _____

Subs:        _____        Subs:        _____

Decisions:   _____        Decisions:   _____

## FIGHT NUMBER 17

## GLADIATOR CHALLENGE AT THE SOBOBA CASINO (VISION QUEST)

**QUESTION 161:** Prior to his fight with Ron Waterman at PRIDE 27, this man pulled a prank on commentator Mauro Ranallo by acting angry towards him for previous comments during an interview. The prank went on for a good three or four minutes and Ranallo was obviously scared by the fighter's stone-faced stares. Finally he was let off the hook and somebody asked if he was scared. "Of course I was ... the way he looked at me I thought he was going to punch me out ... do I get danger pay too?"
- a) Mirko Cro Cop Filipovic
- b) Fedor Emelianenko
- c) Bas Rutten
- d) Kevin Randleman

**QUESTION 162:** This early-days UFC fighter famously said, "We have a saying back home that if you're coming on ... come on!" Much more recently, in December of 2009, he was arrested after a series of incidents that ended when he drove his vehicle into the front of the Fallsview Casino.
- a) Steve Jennum
- b) Joe Son
- c) Keith Hackney
- d) Harold Howard

**QUESTION 163:** This MMA star made his debut at UFC 13. He was still in college and entered the event without a contract and did not get paid.
- a) Randy Couture
- b) Tito Ortiz
- c) Vitor Belfort
- d) Guy Mezger

**QUESTION 164:** While coaching at the University of Nebraska, Matt Lindland won three MMA fights in 1997. Two of them came on the same afternoon at IFC 6 in North Dakota on September 20, when he beat Mark Waters and Travis Fulton. Matt earned a title for the two wins, but never received a belt. Interestingly, the event was held...

- a) at eight in the morning to kick off a local festival in New Town
- b) in an ice skating rink with the cage placed on top of the ice
- c) outside and the temperature was a balmy 30 degrees, but as Matt said, "The sun was out so it was a nice day."
- d) in conjunction with a rock concert and a huge blackjack tournament in the Four Bears Casino's expansive ballrooms

QUESTION 165: Rich Franklin entered his bout at UFC 64 against Anderson Silva with a titanium plate and seven screws in his left hand after breaking his second metacarpal.

Courtesy of Rich Franklin.

He also suffered a hairline fracture in his foot, and tendon damage in his ankle. The injuries came during his second middleweight title defense against David Loiseau at this event.

No doubt he's a warrior and by all accounts a class act. Rich beat David at...
- a) UFC 53
- b) UFC 55
- c) UFC 58
- d) UFC 61

Courtesy of Rich Franklin.

**QUESTION 166:** It was at this UFC event when 4 to 6 ounce gloves, mouthpieces, and groin protectors were made mandatory. This event was also Maurice Smith's UFC debut and he claimed the heavyweight title from Mark Coleman.
- a) UFC 12
- b) UFC 13
- c) UFC 14
- d) UFC 15

**QUESTION 167:** PRIDE held two events, PRIDE 32 and 33, in the United States. Both were in Las Vegas at this building and Dan Henderson and Mauricio Rua each made appearances on both

cards.
   a)   The Thomas & Mack Center
   b)   The Mandalay Bay
   c)   The MGM
   d)   The Cox Pavilion

QUESTION 168: Famous MMA star Ken Shamrock entered Bob Shamrock's home at the age of 13 and it changed his life. Five years later Ken changed his last name to Shamrock when Bob legally adopted him. What was Ken's last name prior to entering Bob's home?
   a)   Sturtz
   b)   Hagander
   c)   Sharp
   d)   Kilpatrick

QUESTION 169: This man got his nickname because his wrestling coaches always called him "Kid" and then in his first three MMA fights he won by (T)KO, including a six second KO of Aiki Cavanaugh. So "KO Kid" was born and he claimed the King of the Cage middleweight belt by the age of 20. During this time he was doing more than just fighting. After an accident as a kid he had to go through rehab and a cool male nurse helped him out, so he decided to go into nursing and was attending California State University, Northridge. And the fighter-nurse's name is...
   a)   Keith Berry
   b)   Efrain Escudero
   c)   Phil Baroni
   d)   Jake Shields

QUESTION 170: British featherweight star Brad Pickett brought his 17-4 record to the WEC in December of 2009 and faced Kyle Dietz. In the second round Pickett locked Dietz up in a seldom used Peruvian Necktie and forced the tap. The victory was named submission of the night and put an extra ten thousand dollars (equivalent to about 39 British pounds in late 2009) in Pickett's wallet. The origins of the Peruvian Necktie can be attributed to this

man, who actually happens to be Peruvian, go figure...
   a)  Kenny Florian
   b)  Andre Pederneiras
   c)  Tony DeSouza
   d)  Gegard Mousasi

# ANSWER KEY FOR FIGHT NUMBER 17
## (VISION QUEST)

QUESTION 161: A          QUESTION 166: C
QUESTION 162: D          QUESTION 167: A
QUESTION 163: B          QUESTION 168: D
QUESTION 164: C          QUESTION 169: A
QUESTION 165: C          QUESTION 170: C

## FIGHT RESULTS

10 for 10      = Sub win via Peruvian Necktie
9 for 10       = Head kick KO victory
8 for 10       = Unanimous decision victory
7 for 10       = Split decision victory
6 for 10       = Split decision loss
5 for 10       = Unanimous decision loss
4 or fewer     = KO'd by a liver shot

## FIGHT RECORD

Wins: _____          Losses: _____

KO's: _____          KO's: _____

Subs: _____          Subs: _____

Decisions: _____          Decisions: _____

## FIGHT NUMBER 18

## EXTREME CHALLENGE AT THE TROPICANA CASINO IN ATLANTIC CITY (THE WAR AT THE SHORE)

**QUESTION 171:** It was at Dynamite!! 2009 on December 31 when DREAM champ Shinya Aoki submitted this man by twisting his arm up behind him in a hammerlock and mercilessly snapping it. He then got into the downed fighters face and flipped him the Tokyo Heybuddy as the guys at Cagepotato.com called it.
   a)   Tatsuya Kawajiri
   b)   Mizuto Hirota
   c)   Eddie Alvarez
   d)   Joachim Hansen

**QUESTION 172:** At UFC 47 when Mike Goldberg asked this fighter, "Who's the harder puncher?" He replied, "Chuck never really got a chance to hit me, but obviously he's got devastating knock out power..." Then Rogan asked, "Did Tito ever connect with you?" And this fighter replied, "No he never hit me either." Rogan said, "Check you out!"
   a)   Quinton Jackson
   b)   Kevin Randleman
   c)   Randy Couture
   d)   Wanderlei Silva

**QUESTION 173:** At the age of ten, Antonio Rodrigo Nogueira suffered severe injuries that left him in a coma for almost four days and in the hospital for months. He has a scar on his back from the incident. What happened?
   a)   a building collapsed on him during an earthquake
   b)   he was attacked by an alligator
   c)   he fell out of a three story window
   d)   he was run over by a truck

**QUESTION 174:** This man was *NOT* in Rob Schneider's prison

comedy (is there such a thing?) *Big Stan.*
   a)   Randy Couture
   b)   Bob Sapp
   c)   Georges St. Pierre
   d)   Don Frye

**QUESTION 175:** After UFC 100, one of Brock Lesnar's cornermen questioned as to why he and the others weren't allowed in the Octagon. He thought that they could have helped settle Lesnar down. If they'd been allowed into the Octagon, which man would *not have* entered because he was *not* in Lesnar's corner at UFC 100?
   a)   Sean Sherk
   b)   Erik Paulson
   c)   Marty Morgan
   d)   Greg Nelson

**QUESTION 176:** In an interview at Cage Potato Tom Lawlor talked of the very deadly fighting art of which he trained. He was asked if we should be concerned about the prospects of Aaron Simpson leaving the Octagon alive after UFN 20. "No, probably not," Lawlor said. "Honestly, my goal when I go into the cage is never to hurt my opponent. I am a proponent of mass efficiency. If you watch the majority of my fights, against Kyle Kingsbury in the UFC, I don't think I threw one punch. Against C.B. Dollaway, I threw a punch, but it didn't hit him. So I'm kind of against violence, actually." His deadly fighting art is called...
   a)   Harold Howard's Jiu Jitsu/Karate Combination
   b)   RIP
   c)   Baboo Baby
   d)   Ring-a-ding-ding-smash

**QUESTION 177:** It was at The Ultimate Fighter 5 Finale when Gray Maynard and this man ended up having a crazy no contest when Gray slammed him and he tapped, but the referee thought Gray knocked himself out in the process. Gray said of the fight, "It taught me fighting is a controlled sport and anytime you let yourself get too amped up or out of control there's a big opportunity to make mistakes, which is what happened that night. I was really disappointed that I didn't get a win in my UFC debut. I went back to the gym and trained really hard for my next fight. I actually started

training again when I got back to the locker room after the fight."
The no contest came against...
   a)   Rob Emerson
   b)   Joe Veres
   c)   Josh Powell
   d)   Dennis Siver

Courtesy of Gray Maynard.

**QUESTION 178:** According to legend (and a video on the Internet) Tank Abbott is a pretty strong dude. He bench pressed what was reported as this amount of weight and yes he bounced it off his chest and yes it would not have been green lighted in a power-lifting competition, but still...
   a)   485 pounds
   b)   545 pounds
   c)   600 pounds
   d)   900 pounds including two bikini models and a Chihuahua

**QUESTION 179:** This lightweight/featherweight American Top Team fighter was arrested in October of 2007 in Port St. Lucie,

Florida for holding "illegal fights" in his gym. It was later determined that the fights were not for profit – they were merely learning experiences for his students so all charges were dropped.
   a)   Din Thomas
   b)   Gesias Cavalcante
   c)   Yves Edwards
   d)   Jorge Masvidal

**QUESTION 180:** Middleweight Logan Clark compiled a 10-0 record including a victory at UFC Fight Night 7 over Steve Byrnes. He then struggled, going just 1-4 in his next five bouts. The Eyota, Minnesota native goes by this interesting nickname that his brothers gave him years ago. Reportedly he used to wear a pink shirt to the cage that read, "Where in the hell is Eyota, MN" … and then he'd beat up his opponents.
   a)   The Pink Flamingo
   b)   The Pink Typhoon
   c)   The Pink Panther
   d)   The Pink Pounder

## ANSWER KEY FOR FIGHT NUMBER 18
## (THE WAR AT THE SHORE)

QUESTION 171: B          QUESTION 176: C
QUESTION 172: C          QUESTION 177: A
QUESTION 173: D          QUESTION 178: C
QUESTION 174: C          QUESTION 179: A
QUESTION 175: A          QUESTION 180: D

## FIGHT RESULTS

10 for 10      = KO win by jaw-rocking uppercut
9 for 10       = Sub victory by Gogoplata
8 for 10       = Unanimous decision victory
7 for 10       = Split decision victory
6 for 10       = Split decision loss
5 for 10       = Unanimous decision loss
4 or fewer     = KO'd by knees in the clinch

## FIGHT RECORD

Wins: _____          Losses: _____

KO's: _____          KO's: _____

Subs: _____          Subs: _____

Decisions: _____          Decisions: _____

# FIGHT NUMBER 19

## ELITE XC IN CORPUS CHRISTI
## (STREET CERTIFIED)

QUESTION 181: Not long before his UFC debut at UFC 18, Bas Rutten was in this trendy bar in Sweden when according to him he was harassed by the bouncers and had a fight with a handful of them. They beat on him with sticks while he dropped one after the other. He was arrested for the incident, but thanks to a friend it wasn't such a big deal and he said he was eating cookies and drinking coffee and tea while watching TV in his cell. He also wrote of the incident:

> *I called my wife before everything happened, when I was in a restaurant eating and drinking. She asked me why I was so happy on the phone. I told here that I had a good time there in Sweden. She said, "Yeah right, you probably have two Swedish girls there with you."*
> *I said, "No baby, I am just having a good time."*
> *Then when I was allowed to make my first phone call in jail, I called my wife, I said, "I have some good news and some bad, what do you want to hear first?"*
> *She said, "The good news."*
> *I said, "OK, I didn't f-*** two Swedish girls."*
> *She said, "What is the bad news?"*
> *I said, "I'm in jail." She didn't really appreciate my joke I guess.*

The name of the bar was...
a) Club Kharma
b) Raw Fusion
c) The Spy Bar
d) The Golden Hits Bar

QUESTION 182: Let's stay on nightclub fights. After beating Charlie Valencia at King of the Cage Predator in May of 2006, this MMA star decided to take a vacation to Bali, Indonesia. The vacation was great until one of the last nights when he ended up in a confrontation at a bar. The guy wanted to fight so he obliged and busted his shoulder up by throwing him into a cement planter. Then he was sucker punched by a guy with brass knuckles and ended up fighting up to 12 Balinese gangsters. He went into the club but found no help and after beating up guys on the dance floor he had to run. He made it outside and dove into a Billabong shop only to get cornered. He fake-begged and then blasted a guy who was carrying a hammer and bolted back to the club. He dove into a taxi and after another scuffle he and the driver got away. This fighter said that he learned a valuable lesson, "Don't f-*** with the Balinese people and it takes more than 12 Balinese with weapons to kill..."

- a) "Pitbull" Andrei Arlovski
- b) Bas "El Guapo" Rutten
- c) "The California Kid" Urijah Faber
- d) "The War Machine" John Koppenhaver

**QUESTION 183:** Okay, one more bar fight question, not long before Lee Murray became a fugitive for his alleged masterminding of the largest bank heist in U.K. history, he was stabbed in a bar fight. The incident took place outside of this bar and had Murray fighting for his life as an artery was severed and a lung was punctured. Reportedly he had to be resuscitated numerous times. The name of the club was...

- a) The Funky Buddha
- b) Storm
- c) Tiger Tiger
- d) Turnmills

**QUESTION 184:** Okay, this really is the last bar fight question ... seriously. These brothers got in a scrap with the bouncers of a dance club after one of them didn't have change to pay the toilet attendant and said he'd pay a Euro when he came back (*B.S. that you have to pay to use the toilet in Europe*). The bouncers jumped all over this minor thing and the brothers ended up sending five of them to the hospital after one of them tagged one of the brothers in the face with a flashlight. Unfortunately, one of the fighting siblings was cut on his hand and it got infected, forcing him out of action for

much of 2009.
   a)   The Emelianenko's
   b)   The Overeem's
   c)   The Rua's
   d)   The Nogueira's

QUESTION 185: How about a fight in an actual cage! It was at UFC 79 when former Navy Seabee Rich Clementi submitted this man, who'd entered the Octagon and promptly gave Clementi the finger. Rich then stood over him after the rear naked choke and the beaten man didn't like it so much and was ready to fight some more. It was an interesting scrap that resulted in Rich's third win in the UFC, and if they would've seen each other in a bar afterward, they probably would've fought...
   a)   Ross Pointon
   b)   Anthony Johnson
   c)   Terry Etim
   d)   Melvin Guillard

QUESTION 186: At the age of 51 this man entered the UFC Octagon and lost to Royce Gracie. A week prior to the fight he severely damaged his ankle but fought anyway. He's also been in numerous movies and television shows and is still the oldest to ever compete in the Octagon.
   a)   Dan Severn
   b)   Oleg Taktarov
   c)   Ron Van Clief
   d)   Keith Hackney

QUESTION 187: During sweeps week in November of 2004, the popular show *Blind Date* teamed up with the UFC to have popular UFC fighters appear as special guests. Which fighter did *NOT* appear on the show?
   a)   Tim Sylvia
   b)   Josh Thomson
   c)   Frank Mir
   d)   Tiki Ghosn

QUESTION 188: At PRIDE Bushido 13, Denis Kang defeated Akihiro Gono in the semifinals of the 2006 Welterweight Grand Prix, but tore his bicep in the process. "I knew it was messed up," he said. "I had a lump the size of a golf ball sticking out from under the skin. I remember looking at my manager and coach and saying, 'No matter what, I'm still fighting.' What can I say, I'd worked so hard to make it in this tournament, you would have had to kill me to stop me." He then fought in the finals with his bicep all rolled up and basically unable to use his right arm and lost a controversial decision to this man.

a)  Gegard Mousasi
b)  Paulo Filho
c)  Dan Henderson
d)  Kazuo Misaki

Denis Kang – courtesy of Martin McNeil.

QUESTION 189: On June 23, 2007 at Cage Fury Fighting Championships 5, Bob Canobbio, of Compubox, used Compustrike at a live MMA event for the first time. The card also had another first as Kevin "Kimbo Slice" Ferguson submitted this former boxer in an exhibition match.

a)  Ray Mercer
b)  Francois Botha
c)  Shannon Briggs
d)  James Toney

QUESTION 190: After a tough start in the UFC, this fighter knew he needed to win against TUF star Phillipe Nover. In an interview at UFC.com he said, "...With Phillipe, I had a feeling he would not want to be in that type of fight with me, so I really wanted to push it and not make it a kickboxing match or a technical jiu-jitsu match. I wanted to make it a brawl, and I figured if I could get him into a brawl, I could beat him." It worked as he scored the TKO in just 63 seconds.

    a)   Efrain Escudero
    b)   Kyle Bradley
    c)   Roli Delgado
    d)   Cole Miller

## ANSWER KEY FOR FIGHT NUMBER 19
### (STREET CERTIFIED)

QUESTION 181: C          QUESTION 186: C
QUESTION 182: C          QUESTION 187: C
QUESTION 183: A          QUESTION 188: D
QUESTION 184: B          QUESTION 189: A
QUESTION 185: D          QUESTION 190: B

## FIGHT RESULTS

| | |
|---|---|
| 10 for 10 | = Sub win via Crucifix |
| 9 for 10 | = Spinning back fist KO |
| 8 for 10 | = Unanimous decision victory |
| 7 for 10 | = Split decision victory |
| 6 for 10 | = Split decision loss |
| 5 for 10 | = Unanimous decision loss |
| 4 or fewer | = Subbed by D'arce choke |

## FIGHT RECORD

Wins: _____          Losses: _____

KO's: _____          KO's: _____

Subs: _____          Subs: _____

Decisions: _____          Decisions: _____

## FIGHT NUMBER 20

## THE BIG STAGE AT THE MANDALAY BAY
## (FISTFUL OF DOLLARS)

QUESTION 191: This UFC personality is also a semi-pro poker player and has cashed in on numerous poker events, including a 158th place finish out of 1,646 players in event 11 of the 2009 World Series of Poker.
  a)  Bruce Buffer
  b)  Jacob "Stitch" Duran
  c)  Joe Rogan
  d)  Dana White

QUESTION 192: In an article in *Fighters Only* magazine the 13-0 Lyle Beerbohm tells the story of how his 70-year-old mother helped him with the nickname "Fancy Pants."
  a)  when he was a kid she bought him some 1970s style striped pants and he wore them all the time because they were his "fancy pants"
  b)  as a kid his mom always told him not to play in his "fancy pants" or they'd get holes in them
  c)  his mom sews and he found a couple different kinds of crazy pants that she owned, so he asked her to make him a pair of fancy pants – she made a crazy pair of colorful pants and the nickname came from that
  d)  in high school Lyle liked to break dance and his mother used to say to him, "you think you're Mr. Fancy Pants when you dance like that"

QUESTION 193: Cristiane "Cyborg" Santos was introduced to MMA by her husband, Evangelista "Cyborg" Santos, and she fought just 18 months after entering the gym. It turned out to be a good move as heading into 2010 she is regarded as the best female fighter in the world. Before MMA she participated in this sport.
  a)  Handball
  b)  Bowling
  c)  Volleyball
  d)  Surfing

QUESTION 194: Keeping with the "Cyborg's," back in February of 2006 at Cage Rage 15, Evangelista was in an absolutely incredible slugfest with this feared striker. He ended up on the wrong end of a late second round KO but it was one of those fights where people say, "There really wasn't a loser," and it even showed up on some lists for one of the best fights of the decade. Evangelista's opponent was...

    a)   Igor Vovchanchyn
    b)   Melvin Manhoef
    c)   Mauricio Rua
    d)   Mark Epstein

QUESTION 195: It was this man, along with Marcus Silveira and Dan Lambert who founded American Top Team in 2003 in Coconut Creek, Florida. The gym has produced numerous world-class fighters and is considered one of the best in the world.

    a)   Murilo Bustamante
    b)   Ricardo Liborio
    c)   Carlson Gracie
    d)   Mario Sperry

QUESTION 196: This man actually founded his own martial art, Gaidojutsu, which combines wrestling and judo locks. He then further developed it by adding striking techniques and submissions and it seems to be working pretty well for him considering all of the UFC champs and contenders that train at his gym.

    a)   Eddie Bravo
    b)   Greg Nelson
    c)   Mark DellaGrotte
    d)   Greg Jackson

QUESTION 197: Another gym question, this former world class kickboxer now has numerous gyms in Milwaukee that has produced a number of talented UFC stars and is considered one of the best Muay Thai trainers outside of Thailand.

    a)   Mark Dellagrotte
    b)   Duke Roufus
    c)   Shawn Tompkins
    d)   Howard Davis Jr.

QUESTION 198: TUF 7 alum and Tulsa, Oklahoma native Gerald Harris once fought just seven days after learning that Corey, his oldest brother and a member of the military, was killed in a motorcycle accident. Gerald prepared a memorial service for friends in Oklahoma while the rest of the family traveled to Georgia where the tragic accident took place. On the day of his fight, a snowstorm kept his family away and according to the MMA Junkie article Gerald didn't even have a trainer to wrap his hands. He still won by KO and then said to the crowd, "Everybody, I've got to let ya'll know my brother just passed away seven days ago. He never got to see me fight in person, but he got to see me fight tonight." Surely his brother saw him fight again when he made his official UFC debut at UFN 20 on January 11, 2010 and scored a TKO over this man and earned KOTN and a $30,000 bonus for his efforts.

a) John Salter
b) Rory MacDonald
c) Michael Guymon
d) Jesse Lennox

QUESTION 199: Pretty much all of us have fond memories of UFC Octagon girl Rachelle Leah, but if you know this you're probably some kind of sicko. It's been quite some time since she made her last lap around the apron. As a matter of fact, the last time she worked as an Octagon girl was during this event, and Rashad Evans bested Jason Lambert on the card.

a) UFC 33
b) UFN 5
c) UFC 63
d) UFC 73

QUESTION 200: An article at *Fighters Only* talks of how this MMA star was influenced by *The Book of Five Rings* and the *Dragonball Z* comic books. He has an eclectic group of heroes as well, from Albert Einstein to Muhammad Ali to Batman. He got his first MMA win in his second fight when he armbarred Erik Paulson in under a minute at Vale Tudo Japan. He also had breakfast with Renzo Gracie one day and then beat him by decision at PRIDE Bushido 1

the next day.
- a) Carlos Newton
- b) Kazushi Sakuraba
- c) Akira Shoji
- d) B.J. Penn

## ANSWER KEY FOR FIGHT NUMBER 20
## (FISTFUL OF DOLLARS)

QUESTION 191: A          QUESTION 196: D
QUESTION 192: C          QUESTION 197: B
QUESTION 193: A          QUESTION 198: A
QUESTION 194: B          QUESTION 199: C
QUESTION 195: B          QUESTION 200: A

## FIGHT RESULTS

10 for 10        = KO win by flurry of punches
9 for 10         = Sub win via kneebar
8 for 10         = Unanimous decision victory
7 for 10         = Split decision victory
6 for 10         = Split decision loss
5 for 10         = Unanimous decision loss
4 or fewer       = KO'd by short left hook

## FIGHT RECORD

Wins:       _____          Losses:      _____

KO's:       _____          KO's:        _____

Subs:       _____          Subs:        _____

Decisions:  _____          Decisions:   _____

Ranger Up's Respect for the Roman
Legionnaire...

# Round Five

You've reached the top. You're fighting on the big stage and you know you have to win to stay. This is it, time to win the belt and keep it.

# ...and those Leading the Charge

# SPQR AND PRIMUS PILUS

THERE HAVE ALWAYS BEEN WARRIORS, men willing to engage in combat with death as a possible consequence. Some have fought for fame, some for fortune, some for land, and some for the good of those that do not fight.

The Roman Legionnaire was as fierce as they come and he was part of a greater Army that used its formations, discipline, and strategies to bring hell on those who stood in its way. However, the Roman Legions gathered just as much strength from their motto Senatus Populusque Romanus, or SPQR, which translates to The Senate and the People of Rome. The warriors believed that they were fighting for the people. They were fighting for the good of Rome, and because of this belief they fought with indomitable spirit.

The Roman Legions were no doubt formidable, but some warriors earned elite status. Their discipline, skill, determination, and deadliness were unmatched. Yet they needed a man to lead them into battle. He was the Primus Pilus, meaning his century was the first file of the first cohort, and he was the one that the enemy first laid eyes upon.

The Primus Pilus was an honor bestowed on a select few and they led the charge for the good of the people.

Today we are seeing modern sport fighters, often referred to as "warriors" or "gladiators" fighting for a chance to be right behind the Primus Pilus. Or better yet to be him, the man in the position for which all others strive, in the front and riding hard into the fight. He may find fame, even fortune as he rides, but if he is leading the charge out of a passion for discipline, a desire to test his worthiness, and with the honor and character of warriors past in his blood, then he can truly be called the Primus Pilus.

## FIGHT NUMBER 21

## THE BIG STAGE AT ARCO ARENA IN SACRAMENTO (ALL THE KING'S MEN)

**QUESTION 201:** UFC 33 was the first MMA event sanctioned by the Nevada State Athletic Commission and it was also now famous cutman Jacob "Stitch" Duran's first day on the job. He arrived a few hours early and the UFC's only cutman at the time, Leon Tabbs, showed him the difference between a boxing wrap (which Stitch had become in demand for) and an MMA wrap. Stitch asked a few questions and then headed down the hall to wrap Dave Menne's and then Jens Pulver's hands. They both then went out and won their championship fights. Menne became the first-ever UFC middleweight title holder and Jens Pulver defended his lightweight title against this man.
   a)   Caol Uno
   b)   Dennis Hallman
   c)   B.J. Penn
   d)   John Lewis

**QUESTION 202:** During each UFC event and prior to it going live to pay per view this song is blasted through the arena while great highlights of some of the best fights and fighters in UFC history are shown. It does a great job of getting the live audience fired up.
   a)   *I'm Shipping up to Boston* by Dropkick Murphys
   b)   *Slam* by Onyx
   c)   *Baba O'Riley* by The Who
   d)   *Are You Ready* by AC/DC

**QUESTION 203:** The *USA Today* did a poll in which fans voted on the top sports breakout of the decade. The mainstream emergence of Mixed Martial Arts crushed the field garnering 47% of the votes. An example of MMA's mainstream emergence can be found in this kids show. In August of 2009 it did a special in which the main character participated in an MMA fight against the rival. The kids/tween show did a remarkable 7.9 million viewers and broke a record for

the show's most watched special.
a)  *The Wizards of Waverly Place*
b)  *Hannah Montana*
c)  *iCarly*
d)  *The Suite Life of Zack and Cody*

**QUESTION 204:** Tim Kennedy trained at The Pit in San Luis Obispo, and with Chuck Liddell in his corner at Extreme Challenge 50 in February of 2003 he stormed through three opponents: Jason Miller, Ryan Narte, and this man who won his first two fights of the evening in a combined 2:19. As crazy as it sounds, Tim might not be the toughest Kennedy in the family, he really wants a BMW F-series, but his wife won't let him have one. Who'd he beat in the third fight at EC 50?
a)  Cruz Chacon
b)  Hector Urbina
c)  Dante Rivera
d)  Chuck Norris

Courtesy of Tim Kennedy.

QUESTION 205: Staying with Tim, after winning the aforementioned fights he joined the Army in January of 2004 and became a Green Beret and deployed in support of Operation Iraqi Freedom and Operation Enduring Freedom multiple times. Among his multiple awards is the Army's Bronze Star medal, which was awarded for valor under fire. Due to one of these deployments, where he wrote about saving a Pomegranate Tree after a three-day firefight, he didn't get to enter the cage in 2008. But he gave a warning to his future opponents regarding his return: *I'll be 100% ready and focused. Even worse for that next opponent, he will have to deal with me imagining that he just stole my last pomegranate. It might seem funny to some of you, but when you have been deployed where I've been and seen what I've seen you realize a single piece of fruit is a really big deal … and that guy across the cage just took mine.* The first guy to "Take Tim's Pomegranate" was this man at Strikeforce Challengers Series 2 and Tim submitted him due to punches in round two.
   a)  Zak Cummings
   b)  Ryan McGivern
   c)  Elias Rivera
   d)  Nick Thompson

QUESTION 206: This UFC star got his nickname because of his Pitbull Terrier and his intense work ethic in the gym. As he tells the story, "I got Hank in college. My parents still lived in Las Vegas so I would come home in the summer time. I had a friend that owned Hank and some other Pitbulls. I went over to his house and saw Hank had blood on him from a dogfight and always had to stay outside in the heat with no shade. I asked why they didn't take care of him better and it seemed like they didn't really care about Hank. They liked the other dogs better and took care of them better. So I asked to take him on a walk and never brought him back."
   a)  Anthony "Rumble" Johnson
   b)  Gray "The Bully" Maynard
   c)  Thiago "The Pitbull" Alves
   d)  Jon "Bones" Jones

QUESTION 207: This UFC star was in Philadelphia for UFC 101 and he appeared on Danny Bonaduce's morning show on 94WYSP along with Matt Serra. During the show he actually punched Bonaduce, at his urging, repeatedly until knocking him down. Serra

stood behind him to prevent injury from the fall and Bonaduce bounced up and told this fighter, "Thank you so much."
   a)  Chuck Liddell
   b)  B.J. Penn
   c)  Mark Coleman
   d)  Tito Ortiz

QUESTION 208: At PRIDE 1 there was one fight under kickboxing rules. It was between Ralph White and this kickboxer and ended because White was on the ground when he was blasted in the forehead. The kick left quite a lump and Bas Rutten said, "It looks like an alien is going to pop out of his head or something." After much discussion where White's cornerman, Dale "Apollo" Cook, argued that the fight should end in a DQ, the fighters embraced and later it was ruled a no contest. At PRIDE 2 this same kickboxer who left the "alien" on White's head returned in an MMA fight and was DQ'd after grabbing the ropes to avoid a takedown against Mark Kerr.
   a)  Ernesto Hoost
   b)  Branko Cikatic
   c)  Jerome Le Banner
   d)  Peter Aerts

QUESTION 209: Rickson Gracie once beat this man on a beach in Rio de Janeiro. He did so because the man had been insulting the Gracie family. There is even grainy footage of the fight on the Internet.
   a)  Marcelo Raul
   b)  Marco Ruas
   c)  Hugo Duarte
   d)  Casemiro Nascimento Martins

QUESTION 210: This man defeated Hodgkin's disease and won an Olympic gold medal at the 1984 games in Los Angeles. Years later he worked as UFC commentator from UFC 4 to UFC 32. He is now a wrestling coach and motivational speaker and has been involved in the fight for MMA legislation in New York.
   a)  Jeff Blatnick
   b)  Bruce Baumgartner
   c)  Steve Fraser
   d)  Mark Schultz

## ANSWER KEY FOR FIGHT NUMBER 21
## (ALL THE KING'S MEN)

| | |
|---|---|
| QUESTION 201: B | QUESTION 206: B |
| QUESTION 202: C | QUESTION 207: D |
| QUESTION 203: C | QUESTION 208: B |
| QUESTION 204: A | QUESTION 209: C |
| QUESTION 205: D | QUESTION 210: A |

## FIGHT RESULTS

(TAKE NOTICE – AFTER 20 FIGHTS THE COMPETITION IS TOUGHER, AND FROM THIS POINT FORWARD WINNING IS MORE DIFFICULT.)

| | |
|---|---|
| 10 for 10 | = Sub win via flying armbar |
| 9 for 10 | = KO win with a straight right |
| 8 for 10 | = Decision victory |
| 7 for 10 | = Split decision loss |
| 6 for 10 | = Unanimous decision loss |
| 5 or fewer | = Subbed by a triangle choke |

## FIGHT RECORD

| | | | |
|---|---|---|---|
| Wins: | ____ | Losses: | ____ |
| KO's: | ____ | KO's: | ____ |
| Subs: | ____ | Subs: | ____ |
| Decisions: | ____ | Decisions: | ____ |

## FIGHT NUMBER 22

## THE BIG STAGE AT THE STAPLES CENTER IN LOS ANGELES (BOTOX, BIG BOOBS, AND BIGGER STRIKES)

QUESTION 211: American Top Team star Mike Thomas Brown was a standout wrestler at Norwich University. Through 22 fights he'd lost just four times and they came against top fighters: Genki Sudo, Joe Lauzon, Hermes Franca, and the fourth loss was against this man when Brown's left knee was severely dislocated during a kneebar. He recovered to grab a submission win just nine months later and was back on the winning track.
   a) Cole Miller
   b) Urijah Faber
   c) Masakazu Imanari
   d) Renato Tavares

QUESTION 212: This man debuted at UFC 4 and then just under three years later he fought Kimo Leopoldo to a draw during PRIDE's inaugural event, making him the first man to fight in both promotions.
   a) Kazushi Sakuraba
   b) Gary Goodridge
   c) Oleg Taktarov
   d) Dan Severn

QUESTION 213: In 2009, Team Sityodtong fighter and UFC veteran Jorge Rivera got back to his winning ways by first scoring a decision over Nissen Osterneck and then TKO'ing this man at UFC 104. The two victories improved the middleweight's record to 17-7 overall and 6-5 in the UFC.
   a) Kendall Grove
   b) Rob Kimmons
   c) Edwin DeWees
   d) Terry Martin

Courtesy of Jorge Rivera.

**QUESTION 214:** Alan Belcher won submission of the night at UFC 93 over Denis Kang, was awarded fight of the night at UFC 100 in a loss to Yoshihiro Akiyama, and then claimed another fight of the night at UFC 107 against this man. It was a heck of a run for him in 2009 and the bonuses totaled $205,000.

    a)   Wilson Gouveia
    b)   Jason Lambert
    c)   Kalib Starnes
    d)   Ed Herman

**QUESTION 215:** Staying with Alan Belcher, he had his first amateur MMA fight at the age of 14. He happened upon some fights at the Timeout Sports Club in Paragould, Arkansas and lied about his age so he could fight. He met up with a grown man named Orville Boozer and beat him with an Americana in the second round. After 21 fights Alan was much more experienced than he was against Orville and he had a 15-6 record overall and was 6-4 in the UFC. He calls this gym in Mississippi his home.

    a)   Gladiator Fight Club
    b)   Total BJJ and MMA
    c)   The 11th Planet
    d)   Remix MMA

**QUESTION 216:** In B.J. Penn's second scrap with Matt Hughes, at UFC 63, he looked great until it appeared he gassed in the third round. Hughes punished him in the round until the fight was stopped. It was later learned that B.J. suffered from this type of injury during the fight that caused much of the problems.
   a)   separated ribs
   b)   a partially collapsed lung
   c)   cartilage was torn away from his sternum
   d)   a torn rectus abdominus (stomach) muscle

**QUESTION 217:** Reportedly, this Brit's nickname, "One Punch," comes from Brad Pitt's character Mickey O'Neil in the movie *Snatch*. This may very well be the case, but the "One Punch" moniker might've been bestowed upon him because in his very first pro fight at Cage Rage 9 he TKO'd Stuart Grant in only 17 seconds. Either way, through 22 fights he was an impressive 18-4 and had just won his debut in the WEC in exciting fashion.
   a)   Brad Pickett
   b)   Andre Winner
   c)   Mark Weir
   d)   Tom Watson

**QUESTION 218:** This Team Quest fighter talks of working in the late Evan Tanner's corner during a fight with Homer Moore at UFC 34 after realizing Tanner was basically alone. In the first round Tanner made numerous triangle attempts (his best submission) without any luck. The cornerman told Evan that Moore was too big and that he should fake a triangle and transition into an armbar. "I don't know how to do that," Tanner said. The cornerman replied, "Just do it." About a minute later Evan Tanner had his first armbar submission in 27 fights and it came after faking a triangle. It turned out to be the only armbar win during his career. The cornerman's advice was rock solid because of who he was giving it to. "I knew for sure he was that intelligent of a guy that he'd do it when it came down to crunch time," he said. And the guy who gave the advice was...
   a)   Dan Henderson
   b)   Matt Lindland
   c)   Nate Quarry
   d)   Ed Herman

**QUESTION 219:** After stunning everyone with his stoppage of Rashad Evans at UFC 98, Lyoto Machida said in the post-fight interview with Joe Rogan, "Karate is back..." And he went on to say...

 a) "I have told you and now I have showed you, long live the Machida's!"
 b) "If you have a dream in your life, go ahead. It is possible!"
 c) "Really it never left, but now it is back for good and I will not go away."
 d) "Machida Karate with a healthy dose of daily urine is unstoppable!"

**QUESTION 220:** At UFC 12, this man was set to face Mark Coleman for the promotion's first actual heavyweight title. Big John McCarthy came to his corner and asked if he had any questions. He said something about how fast trains travel and then, "Well you know I've been wondering John, if I travel ten miles an hour, and a train travels at 50 miles an hour, and I gotta travel a 30 minutes distance, how many apples does Mary have left in the basket? Real tough word problem, monkey." (At least it *sounded* like he said monkey, but it was kind of hard to understand...) "Good Luck, you fight smart now," Big John replied. And the fighter with the question was...

 a) Don Frye
 b) Bas Rutten
 c) Maurice Smith
 d) Dan Severn

## ANSWER KEY FOR FIGHT NUMBER 22
### (BOTOX, BIG BOOBS, AND BIGGER STRIKES)

QUESTION 211: C

QUESTION 212: D

QUESTION 213: B

QUESTION 214: A

QUESTION 215: D

QUESTION 216: A

QUESTION 217: A

QUESTION 218: C

QUESTION 219: B

QUESTION 220: D

## FIGHT RESULTS

| | |
|---|---|
| 10 for 10 | = KO win via overhand left |
| 9 for 10 | = Sub win via neck crank |
| 8 for 10 | = Decision victory |
| 7 for 10 | = Split decision loss |
| 6 for 10 | = Unanimous decision loss |
| 5 or fewer | = KO'd by a fade away right |

## FIGHT RECORD

Wins: _____

KO's: _____

Subs: _____

Decisions: _____

Losses: _____

KO's: _____

Subs: _____

Decisions: _____

## FIGHT NUMBER 23

## AT THE MGM GRAND
## (ON THE *BIG* STAGE)

**QUESTION 221:** Fighter Dan Quinn was 5-5-1 through 11 fights and really should be a spokesperson for...
  a)  Notre Dame Football
  b)  Stevia and its benefits when mixed with water in a process called cold fission
  c)  Hair Club for Men
  d)  The Path to Enlightenment

**QUESTION 222:** Denis Kang made his UFC debut at 93 against Alan Belcher with a fractured ankle. His doctor told him not to take the fight, but he said, "I thought, '*ok I'm at least going to try my hardest to rehab it.*' Three weeks from the fight I could box and do BJJ from my back so I decided to take it anyways. It was a mistake but I learnt from it." His next fight happened in his hometown of Montreal and he said, "I loved fighting at home. I remember things like driving my truck and eating in my own kitchen, were all things that seemed surreal to me so close to the fight." It worked well for Denis as he scored a decision over this man at UFC 97.
  a)  Marvin Eastman
  b)  Xavier Foupa-Pokam
  c)  Jason MacDonald
  d)  Rousimar Palhares

**QUESTION 223:** At UFC 1 Art Jimmerson and his corner hatched a plan to throw in the towel as soon as Royce Gracie took him down after sitting backstage and watching some of the early carnage. Jimmerson was taken down, but for this odd reason he ended up having to verbally submit. According to Royce, "He [Art] just give up. He's like, 'Get off me, get off me.' He panicked. I was like, you quit? And he was like, 'Sure, stop, stop!' I was like okay what just happened here." What happened with the towel was...
  a)  a couple of fans had stolen the towels from the corner so they didn't have anything to throw
  b)  in the haste to throw in the towel the corner panicked and actually threw a water bottle that almost hit the referee

c)  the corner did not think that he was really in any trouble
    so they decided to wait a few seconds
d)  the corner threw the towel, but with the arm of a second
    grade girl (no offense second grade girls!) ... it got caught
    on the fence and the referee didn't see it

**QUESTION 224:** In 2008 middleweight MMA star Matt Lindland ran
as a Republican for a seat on the Oregon House of Representatives
with this District. He won the Republican nomination, but lost a
close general election. "Politicians will say anything to win," Matt
said. "They don't care about issues. They only care about winning. I
wasn't willing to sacrifice my principles and values to get votes.
That could've been my downfall." For which district did he run?
  a)  District 8
  b)  District 20
  c)  District 52
  d)  District 99

**QUESTION 225:** At the PRIDE 2000 Grand Prix Finals, Royce Gracie
and Kazushi Sakuraba fought a movie-length bout at 90 minutes, or
six 15-minute rounds. Sakuraba was the winner because Royce's
corner eventually stopped it. Sakuraba was "rewarded" with
another fight against...
  a)  Igor Vovchanchyn
  b)  Guy Mezger
  c)  Wanderlei Silva
  d)  Quinton Jackson

**QUESTION 226:** The seemingly mild-mannered and quiet Fedor
Emelianenko, one of the best fighters in the world, grew up in this
Russian city.
  a)  Stary Oskol
  b)  Vladivostok
  c)  St. Petersburg
  d)  Sosensky

**QUESTION 227:** Toby Imada pulled off a stunning inverted triangle
choke (the name doesn't give it justice) at Bellator Fighting
Championship on May 1, 2009. The finish earned Imada the
*Fighters Only World Mixed Martial Arts 2009* submission of the year

and it came against this fighter, who he was trailing until the tap.
- a)  Alonzo Martinez
- b)  Jorge Masvidal
- c)  Thiago Tavares
- d)  Marcus Aurelio

**QUESTION 228:** It was at this UFC event in Newcastle, England when Paul Taylor and Paul Kelly hooked it up, becoming the first Brits ever to face each other in the Octagon. They came out with an extended flurry that had the crowd on its feet, but in the end it was Paul Kelly who took the battle between the Brits at this event.
- a)  UFC 75
- b)  UFC 80
- c)  UFC 89
- d)  UFC 95

**QUESTION 229:** Sticking with firsts, it is believed (sorry, I'm *not* going to research this one any further) that War Machine is the first-ever fighter to have his butt waxed (and posted it on You Tube) in preparation for his scene with this female adult film star. She said of Mr. Machine, "He admitted to being a bit nervous, which actually made me nervous too. When the camera started, he completely shocked me. He was an animal and a total natural! War Machine is now on the top of my list!"
- a)  Lisa Ann
- b)  Angelina Armani
- c)  Jesse Jane
- d)  Riley Steele

**QUESTION 230:** MTV's Bully Beatdown host Jason "Mayhem" Miller is always entertaining, whether with his comments, entrances, or actual fights. Back in October of 2004 Miller beat Ronald Jhun and then had an incident with this fighter, prompting Miller to say, "...The scumbag sucker punched me. That is not honorable. I am a Samurai. He is a ninja, and not even a cool ninja. He's like one of the foot soldiers on Ninja Turtles. I'm going to tear through him like I have nun chucks." Miller got a chance to fight this man some nine months later and he did tear through him before subbing him with

a Shaka (he gave the hang loose sign) armbar.
- a)   Falaniko Vitale
- b)   Mark Moreno
- c)   Lodune Sincaid
- d)   Egan Inoue

Courtesy of Jason Miller.

## ANSWER KEY FOR FIGHT NUMBER 23
## (ON THE *BIG* STAGE)

QUESTION 221: B          QUESTION 226: A
QUESTION 222: B          QUESTION 227: B
QUESTION 223: D          QUESTION 228: B
QUESTION 224: C          QUESTION 229: D
QUESTION 225: A          QUESTION 230: B

## FIGHT RESULTS

| | |
|---|---|
| 10 for 10 | = Sub win by inverted triangle choke |
| 9 for 10 | = KO win via flying knee |
| 8 for 10 | = Decision victory |
| 7 for 10 | = Split decision loss |
| 6 for 10 | = Unanimous decision loss |
| 5 or fewer | = Subbed by a flying scissor heel hook |

## FIGHT RECORD

Wins:          _____          Losses:          _____

KO's:          _____          KO's:          _____

Subs:          _____          Subs:          _____

Decisions:          _____          Decisions:          _____

# FIGHT NUMBER 24

## UNDER THE LIGHTS AT FENWAY PARK
## (BIG LEAGUE BRAWL ... AND THE YANKEES *SUCK!*)

**QUESTION 231:** Thanks to a whole lot of trash talking, Hermes Franca decided to fight this Manny for only one dollar on October 30, 2004. They'd gone back and forth on the popular MMA forum *The Underground* and finally Hermes had enough. The fight would be one ten minute round and Manny would win if he didn't get KO'd or submitted. It took Hermes just 37 seconds to score the KO and he then wrote on the dollar bill, *Shut up Manny*.
- a) Manny Gamburyan
- b) Manny Tapia
- c) Manny Silveira
- d) Manny Reyes Jr.

**QUESTION 232:** While still deployed, Marine Captain Brian Stann contacted promoters in hopes of landing his first professional fight. Sportfight, operated by Matt Lindland and Randy Couture, gave him a chance and he did not disappoint, scoring a TKO over Aaron Stark. Stann (T)KO'd his first six opponents. The sixth was a fast KO over this man at WEC 33, which gave Stann the WEC light heavyweight belt.
- a) Steve Cantwell
- b) Doug Marshall
- c) Rodney Wallace
- d) Craig Zellner

**QUESTION 233:** It was at this UFC event when headbutts, groin strikes, strikes to the back of the neck and head, kicks to a downed opponent, small joint manipulation, pressure point strikes, and hair pulling all became illegal.
- a) they were always illegal it was just that the promoters didn't want the general public to know
- b) UFC 10
- c) UFC 15
- d) technically pressure point strikes are still not illegal because it was determined by the New Jersey Sate Athletic Control Board that it would not be possible to ascertain if a

fighter was purposefully striking a pressure point area or if the strike was truly having its intended effect

**QUESTION 234:** Former UFC middleweight champ Rich Franklin packed on a lot of muscle at the University of Cincinnati. "I was in a five year program," he said. "I started lifting seriously and educating myself about nutrition during my senior year of high school. I believe nutrition was the key along with being a late bloomer. By the time it was all said and done it was about fifty pounds." Also after it was all said and done he went on to be a high school math teacher for four years at this high school
   a)   St. Xavier
   b)   Anderson
   c)   Oak Hills
   d)   St. Edward all-boys school (he taught Gray Maynard for a semester)

Courtesy of Rich Franklin.

**QUESTION 235:** Staying with Rich, who through 15 appearances in the Octagon was 11-4, he starred alongside Tiffani Thiessen in the movie *Cyborg Soldier.* He said of his co-star, "She was a fun and down to earth girl to work with," and when asked if he brought up *Saved by the Bell* he said, "I tried to stay away from the *Saved by the*

*Bell* topic, I'm sure it is completely old to her." *Cyborg Soldier* was to go by a different name originally. It was going to be called...

    a)  *Weapon*
    b)  *I.S.A.A.C.*
    c)  *Robot Warrior*
    d)  *Human Destroyer*

Courtesy of Rich Franklin.

**QUESTION 236:** This former football star caught 624 passes during his stellar career in the NFL. Then on June 2, 2007 he decided to try his hand in MMA at K-1 Hero's *Dynamite USA*. The event was in the L.A. Coliseum, the same place where the USC star played his home football games. It didn't go well as Bernard Ackah, who also happened to be a stand up comedian, knocked him out in 38 seconds. Mak Takano, who was an integral part of putting the event together at the Coliseum said, "We thought, a perfect debut for him to start his MMA career as he'd been training for years. Also a decent match up as Bernard was a part-time pro fighter without much experience, but in the fight game anything can happen, and it did." Maybe this ex-football star will feel better knowing that Ackah was 4-3 through seven fights with two wins that were faster than

his 38 second KO.
   a)  Johnnie Morton
   b)  Michael Westbrook
   c)  Rex Richards
   d)  Keyshawn Johnson

**QUESTION 237:** Mike Thomas Brown took the WEC featherweight belt from Urijah Faber with a stunning TKO at WEC 36. He defended the belt against Faber at WEC 41 in a tremendous five round affair in which Faber broke his hand in the first round. In between these two fights Brown had another title defense against this man.
   a)  Manny Gamburyan
   b)  Jeff Curran
   c)  Leonard Garcia
   d)  Jens Pulver

**QUESTION 238:** This man handed both Antonio Rodrigo Nogueira and Renato Sobral their first professional MMA losses on the very same night – and for good measure he beat Gilbert Yvel as well.
   a)  Dan Henderson
   b)  Quinton Jackson
   c)  Fedor Emelianenko
   d)  Ricardo Arona

**QUESTION 239:** Renato Sobral had his big night though as well. At IFC in the thin air of Denver, Colorado, Sobral first beat the 6-0 Trevor Prangley by decision. He then subbed 4-0 Mauricio Rua in the third round with a Guillotine, and finished the night by winning a decision over this much more experienced fighter.
   a)  Dan Severn
   b)  Jeremy Horn
   c)  Travis Wiuff
   d)  Travis Fulton

**QUESTION 240:** Dan Hardy and Mike Swick had toured U.S. Military bases together along with Jon Fitch and Octagon girl Edith in early 2009, but in November they were set to fight each other at UFC

105. Dan gave Mike this item at the pre-fight press conference.
   a)   a runner-up trophy
   b)   a pair of Union Jack shorts
   c)   an autographed photo of himself
   d)   a fake Lloyds of London insurance policy

## ANSWER KEY FOR FIGHT NUMBER 24
## (BIG LEAGUE BRAWL ... AND THE YANKEES *SUCK!*)

QUESTION 231: D

QUESTION 232: B

QUESTION 233: C

QUESTION 234: C

QUESTION 235: A

QUESTION 236: A

QUESTION 237: C

QUESTION 238: A

QUESTION 239: B

QUESTION 240: A

## FIGHT RESULTS

| 10 for 10 | = Win by head kick KO |
| 9 for 10 | = Sub win by Gogoplata |
| 8 for 10 | = Decision victory |
| 7 for 10 | = Split decision loss |
| 6 for 10 | = Unanimous decision loss |
| 5 or fewer | = KO'd by an upkick |

## FIGHT RECORD

Wins: _____

Losses: _____

KO's: _____

KO's: _____

Subs: _____

Subs: _____

Decisions: _____

Decisions: _____

## FIGHT NUMBER 25

## THE MECCA – MADISON SQUARE GARDEN ARENA IN NEW YORK CITY
## (GLORY'S LAST CHANCE ... AND BOSTON *SUCKS!*)

**QUESTION 241:** This Louisianan lost his first two fights and began his career just 3-6. He now fights at lightweight, but during those days he was entering the cage at about 225 pounds. He was definitely green as he once said, "It wasn't until my third fight that I finally learned what butterfly guard was!" He for sure knows now and back on February 26, 2005 he blew out his ACL in the first round against Daisuke Hanazawa but gutted out a decision. He ended up using part of his hamstring tendon to replace the torn knee tendon. Through 50 fights he was 34-15-1. This excludes the tag team match between him and Jeff Curran against the Kotani brothers, but includes his decision victory over Naoyuki Kotani in the ZST Grand Prix.
   a) Din Thomas
   b) Rich Clementi
   c) Joe Riggs
   d) Josh Neer

**QUESTION 242:** Bas Rutten was at a charity event after party when he accidentally stepped on the toe of this NFL star. Rutten apologized and offered to buy him a drink. The NFL star would have none of it and asked if he wanted to step outside. "Yes, I would like that very much," Bas replied. Security and friends then informed the football player as to whom he was dealing with and, oddly enough, everything was cool...
   a) Terrell Owens
   b) Adam "Pacman" Jones
   c) Brian Urlacher
   d) Ray Lewis

**QUESTION 243:** This Australian middleweight fighter used to train with and was the bodyguard of TV star "The Crocodile Hunter" Steve Irwin, who died in September of 2006 when he was stung by Stingray. Irvin loved the sport and Greg Jackson had even trained him for years. They were such good friends that Jackson attended Irvin's funeral in Australia.

a) Tony Bonello
b) Elvis Sinosic
c) Kyle Noke
d) Matt Cain

**QUESTION 244:** Lee Murray was a great Brit fighter with huge potential before he decided to go Bonnie and Clyde (okay just Clyde) on us and steal over 50 million pounds. His last fight came in Cage Rage and it was full of drama as Lee lost a decision to this man.

a) Joe Doerksen
b) Anderson Silva
c) Jose Landi-Jons
d) Jorge Rivera

**QUESTION 245:** This UFC lightweight never fought in PRIDE. He almost appeared on the PRIDE 9 card in Nagoya, Japan against Johil de Oliviera, but did not because Oliviera was literally burned by the pre-fight pyrotechnics.

a) Din Thomas
b) Joe Lauzon
c) Spencer Fisher
d) Matt Serra

**QUESTION 246:** Gerald Gordeau gouged the right eye of this Japanese Vale Tudo legend at Vale Tudo Japan 1995, to the point where he is permanently blind in the eye. He went on to submit Gordeau and then with a bandage on his eye, submitted Craig Pittman. Finally, he was submitted by another legend, Rickson Gracie. Because of fear that it would give the sport a bad image, he actually kept the resulting blindness secret for many years.

a) Kazushi Sakuraba
b) Yuki Nakai
c) Genki Sudo
d) Yuki Kondo

**QUESTION 247:** UFC 24 was named *First Defense* in reference to Kevin Randleman's first heavyweight title defense against this man. Unfortunately it didn't happen because while warming up backstage Randleman slipped on the concrete floor and knocked himself out cold. An ambulance (Joe Rogan might call it da amberlamps) rushed him to the hospital and UFC 24 had seven, instead of eight fights. Randleman's scheduled opponent did get a crack at him later.

a) Ricco Rodriguez
b) Randy Couture
c) Pete Williams
d) Pedro Rizzo

QUESTION 248: This famous screenwriter/movie producer was in attendance at UFC 1 and as Brian Kilmeade interviewed Ken Shamrock he mentioned the producer. "...big time movie producer thinks you got an amazing potential. It'd be a lot safer..." Ken laughed and said, "I like fighting."

a) David Mamet
b) John Milius
c) Bobby Razak
d) Jerry Bruckheimer

QUESTION 249: Enson Inoue, a fighter known for his toughness, reportedly spent four days in the hospital with injuries including a cracked jaw, a ruptured eardrum, a broken finger, and brain swelling so bad that the doctor called it critical after he lost to this man.

a) Frank Shamrock
b) Igor Vovchanchyn
c) Antonio Rodrigo Nogueira
d) Mark Kerr

QUESTION 250: Thanks to an early stoppage and an injury to Tank Abbott, this undersized man fought twice at Ultimate Japan and against the same man. He won the second time claiming the heavyweight tournament in the process. He was no doubt an unlikely champ in December of 1997.

a) Vitor Belfort
b) Randy Couture
c) Kazushi Sakuraba
d) Frank Shamrock

## Answer Key for Fight Number 25
## (Glory's Last Chance ... and Boston *Sucks!*)

QUESTION 241: B                    QUESTION 246: B
QUESTION 242: C                    QUESTION 247: D
QUESTION 243: C                    QUESTION 248: B
QUESTION 244: B                    QUESTION 249: B
QUESTION 245: D                    QUESTION 250: C

### Fight Results

| | |
|---|---|
| 10 for 10 | = Sub win by rear naked choke |
| 9 for 10 | = KO win by a straight right |
| 8 for 10 | = Decision victory |
| 7 for 10 | = Split decision loss |
| 6 for 10 | = Unanimous decision loss |
| 5 or fewer | = Subbed by a Guillotine |

### Fight Record

Wins: _____                       Losses: _____

KO's: _____                       KO's: _____

Subs: _____                       Subs: _____

Decisions: _____                  Decisions: _____

# OVERALL RECORD / FINAL RANKING

### 12 OR FEWER WINS
### = YOU'RE A CAN

### 14 WINS AND FOUR OR FEWER LOSSES VIA STOPPAGE
### = YOU'RE A JOURNEYMAN

### 16 WINS AND THREE OR FEWER LOSSES VIA STOPPAGE
### = YOU'RE A GATEKEEPER

### 18 WINS WITH AT LEAST 9 KO'S/SUBS AND TWO OR FEWER LOSSES VIA STOPPAGE
### = YOU'RE A CONTENDER

### 20 WINS WITH AT LEAST 10 KO'S/SUBS AND TWO OR FEWER LOSSES VIA STOPPAGE
### = YOU'RE A CHAMP

### 22 WINS WITH AT LEAST 15 KO'S/SUBS AND NO LOSSES VIA STOPPAGE
### = YOU'RE THE POUND-FOR-POUND CHAMP

### 24 WINS WITH AT LEAST 20 KO'S/SUBS AND NO LOSSES VIA STOPPAGE
### = HALL OF FAMER

### 25 WINS WITH AT LEAST 20 KO'S/SUBS AND NO LOSSES
### = LEGENDARY STATUS AS G.O.A.T. (GREATEST OF ALL-TIME!)

Itching for another fight? Go to www.blackmesabooks.com and visit the Mixed Martial Arts page. Use the "Extra Fights" link to download a free E-Book with brand new questions from MMA author Zac Robinson. To access the link you need the following:

Username: blackmesa
Password: rangerup

## About the Author

Zac Robinson is a former collegiate baseball player who has trained in a variety of Martial Arts. He is passionate about both baseball and combat sports. Zac is also the author of Mixed Martial Arts IQ (Volume I) and he is a co-author of two Sports by the Numbers books, *San Francisco Giants: An Interactive Guide to the World of Sports* and *Mixed Martial Arts: An Interactive Guide to the World of Sports*. Zac also worked with legendary cutman Jacob "Stitch" Duran on his biography, *From Migrant Camp to Madison Square Garden: The Stitch Duran Story*.

You can visit Zac on the web:

www.sportsbythenumbersmma.com
www.cutmanstitchduran.com

## Also by Zac Robinson

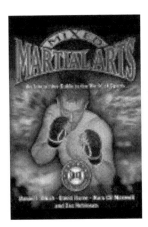

*Mixed Martial Arts IQ: The Ultimate Test of True Fandom (Volume I)*

*Mixed Martial Arts: An Interactive Guide to the World of Sports*

"Every time I work on a cut I am being tested and I feel confident I can pass the test. After reading MMA IQ I'm not so sure I can do the same with this book."
— UFC Cutman Jacob "Stitch" Duran, www.stitchdurangear.com

"MMA fans everywhere pay attention—this is your best chance to reign supreme in your favorite bar stool. The trivia and stories come at you so fast and so furious you'll wish Stitch Duran was in your corner getting you ready to do battle."
— Sam Hendricks, award-winning author of *Fantasy Football Tips: 201 Ways to Win through Player Rankings, Cheat Sheets and Better Drafting*

"From the rookie fan to the pound for pound trivia champs, MMA IQ has something that will challenge the wide spectrum of fans that follow the sport."
— Robert Joyner, www.mmapayout.com

"I thought I knew MMA, but this book took my MMA IQ to a whole new level . . . fun read, highly recommended."
— William Li, www.findmmagym.com

"Fighting is physical storytelling where villains and heroes emerge, but the back-story is what makes the sport something that persisted from B.C. times to what we know it as today. Antonio Rodrigo Nogueira living through a childhood coma only to demonstrate equal grit inside the ring on his way to two world championships. Randy Couture defying age like it was as natural as sunrise on his way to six world championships. The achievements are endless in nature, but thanks to this book, these great human narratives are translated into a universal language—numbers—in a universal medium—fighting."

— Danny Acosta, Sherdog.com and *Fight!* Magazine Writer

"Statistics have long been resigned to slower, contemplative sports. Finally, they get a crack at the world's fastest sport in this fascinating piece of MMA analysis."

— Ben Zeidler, CagePotato.com, *Fight!* Magazine

You can visit Mixed Martial Arts IQ author Zac Robinson on the web:

www.sportsbythenumbersmma.com
www.cutmanstitchduran.com

# References

## BOOKS

*Becoming the Natural: My Life in and Out of the Cage* (Randy Couture with Loretta Hunt)

*From Migrant Camp to Madison Square Garden: the Stitch Duran Story* (Jacob Stitch Duran with Zac Robinson)

*Got Fight? The 50 Zen Principles of Hand-to-Face Combat* (Forrest Griffin with Erich Krauss)

*Iceman: my Fighting Life* (Chuck Liddell with Chad Millman)

*Little Evil: One Ultimate Fighter's Rise to the Top* (Jens Pulver with Erich Krauss)

*Made in America: the Most Dominant Champion in UFC History* (Matt Hughes with Michael Malice)

*Mixed Martial Arts: an Interactive Guide to the World of Sports* (Daniel J. Brush, David Horne, Marc CB Maxwell, and Zac Robinson)

*Title Shot: Into the Sharks Tank of Mixed Martial Arts* (Kelly Crigger)

## INTERVIEWS

Chael Sonnen
Chris Leben
Denis Kang
Gray Maynard
Jacob Stitch Duran
Mak Takano
Matt Lindland
Mo Lawal
Nate Quarry
Patrick Cote
Rich Franklin
Tim Kennedy

## MAGAZINES
*Elite Fighter* (February 2008)
*Fight!* (December/January 2007, February 2008, March 2008, June 2008, August 2009)
*Fighters Only* (Issue 7 September 2009, Issue 10 December 2009)
*MMA Sports* (Issue 19)
*MMA Worldwide* (Issue 9, 2008, Issue 10, 2008, Issue 11, 2008)
*Revista Virtual PVT Magazine*
*TapouT* (Issue 23, 2008)
*UFC Magazine* (Premiere Issue, December/January 2010)

## WEB SITES
Bloodyelbow.com
Cagepotato.com
Compustrike.com
Cortlandstandard.net
ESPN.com
Fcfighter.com
FightersOnly.com
Fightmagazine.com
Findmmaygym.com
MixedMartialArts.com Fighter Database
Mlive.com
MMA.fanhouse.com
MMAjunkie.com
MMApayout.com
Philly.com
Portaldovt.com
Sherdog.com Fight Finder Database
Sportsbythenumbersmma.com
Tapoutlive.com
Thegarv.com
Thevoiceonline.info
UFC.com
USAtoday.com
Yahoosports.com

## OTHER
*Best Damn Sports Show Period* (Bas Rutten Interview)
Commentating of Joe Rogan and Mike Goldberg at UFC events
*The Renzo Gracie Legacy Documentary*

## About Black Mesa

Look for these other titles in the IQ Series:

- *Mixed Martial Arts (Volume I)*
- *Atlanta Braves*
- *New York Yankees*
- *Cincinnati Reds*
- *Milwaukee Brewers*
- *St. Louis Cardinals*
- *Boston Red Sox*
- *Major League Baseball*
- *University of Oklahoma Football*
- *University of Georgia Football*
- *University of Florida Football*
- *Penn State Football*
- *Boston Celtics*
- *University of Kentucky Basketball*
- *University of Louisville Basketball*

For information about special discounts for bulk purchases, please email: black.mesa.publishing@gmail.com

www.blackmesabooks.com

Made in the USA
Lexington, KY
02 May 2010